GLOBETROTTER™

Travel Guide

LANZAROTE

Rowland Mead

NEW HOLLAN

D0937637

NEW
HOLLAND

★★★ Highly recommended
★★ Recommended
★ See if you can

Sixth edition published in 2015
by MapStudio™
10 9 8 7 6 5 4 3 2 1
www.globetrottertravelguides.com

Distributed in Africa by
MapStudio™
Unit3, Block B, M5 Park, Eastman Road,
Maitland 7405, Cape Town, South Africa
PO Box 193, Maitland 7404

Distributed in the UK/Europe/Asia by
John Beaufoy Publishing Ltd

Distributed in the USA by
National Book Network

ISBN 978 1 77026 675 9

This guidebook has been written by independent authors and
updaters. The information therein represents their impartial
opinion, and neither they nor the publishers accept payment
in return for including in the book or writing more favourable
reviews of any of the establishments. Whilst every effort has
been made to ensure that this guidebook is as accurate and
up to date as possible, please be aware that the facts quoted
are subject to change, particularly the price of food, transport
and accommodation. The Publisher accepts no responsibility
or liability for any loss, injury or inconvenience incurred by
readers or travellers using this guide.

Commissioning Editor: Elaine Fick
DTP Cartographic Manager: Genené Hart
Editors: Elaine Fick, Thea Grobbelaar, Melany Porter,
Jacqueline de Vos
Picture Researchers: Shavonne Govender,
Colleen Abrahams
Design and DTP: Nicole Bannister, Lellyn Creamer
Cartographers: Rudi de Lange, Genené Hart, Reneé Spocter,
Lorissa Bouwer, Marisa Roman
Updated in 2015 by: Lindsay Bennett

Reproduction by Hirt & Carter (Pty) Ltd, Cape Town
Printed and bound by Craft Print International Ltd, Singapore

Keep us Current
Information in travel guides is apt to change, which is why
we regularly update our guides. We'd be grateful to receive
feedback if you've noted something we should include in
our updates. If you have new information, please share
it with us by writing to the Commissioning Editor at the
MapStudio address on this page. The most significant
contribution to each new edition will receive a free copy of
the updated guide.

Front Cover: *View over Jardín de Cactus, Guatiza.*
Title Page: *Traditional costumes are worn for festivals.*

CONTENTS

1
Introducing
Lanzarote

Lanzarote, the most easterly island in the Canary archipelago, is in many ways unique. Although all the islands are volcanic, it is on Lanzarote that the volcanic features are most impressive and easily approachable. It is possible to take a bus right to the very top of a volcano that, geologically speaking, has recently erupted and, an hour later, travel over low hills of volcanic ash and cinder on a camel. Within a few kilometres of these 'mountains of fire' there are pretty villages of whitewashed houses, which are surrounded by vines growing in sheltered hollows in the volcanic cinders.

Although all of the Canary Islands have pleasant winter weather, it is Lanzarote that has the most consistent climate. Since it is situated close to Africa (125km/77 miles) with no high mountains, Lanzarote has more sunshine than any other of the islands. Daytime temperatures in January and February are rarely below 22°C (72°F), and rainfall is light and falls on no more than 16 days a year. Not surprisingly, Lanzarote has become a popular winter holiday destination for northern Europeans. They are attracted to the climate and the harmonious nature of the landscape, which is not as developed as the other islands.

César Manrique – artist, sculptor and environmentalist – wielded an enormous influence over Lanzarote's government and is largely responsible for preserving the island's natural state. He was well aware of the destructive consequences that tourism can bring and was determined to keep the island from being spoiled. As a result, nearly two-thirds of

TOP ATTRACTIONS

*** Timanfaya National Park: see volcanic splendour in the 'Mountains of Fire'.
** Jameos del Agua: view a partly collapsed volcanic tube, with a subterranean lake.
** Cueva de los Verdes: take a 2km (1.2-mile) guided walk through a lava cave.
** Mirador del Río: clifftop viewpoint and restaurant overlooking Isla Graciosa.
* Teguise: see elegant buildings and a vibrant Sunday market in the former capital.
* Fundación César Manrique: visit an art gallery in Manrique's former home.

◄ *Opposite: An artificial geyser in Timanfaya National Park.*

INTRODUCING LANZAROTE

Lanzarote is free from tourist establishments and where development has taken place, respect for local customs and traditions is evident. Manrique's influence can be seen everywhere, from roadside sculptures to restaurants that blend harmoniously into volcanic lava. Few buildings are taller than a Canary palm tree and roadside hoardings are banned.

The unique combination of the mild temperature, well-preserved landscape and the might of the volcanoes is appealing to discriminating tourists and many return year after year. Lanzarote now has 1.9 million tourists annually (2013 figures) spread evenly throughout the year. Nearly a half of these come from the United Kingdom and a quarter from Germany. All receive a warm welcome from *Lanzaroteños*. It is perhaps not surprising that in 1993 UNESCO designated the whole island as a Biosphere Reserve.

THE LAND

Lanzarote is one of the **Canary Islands**, an archipelago lying approximately 300km (186 miles) west of the African coast of Morocco. The islands belong to Spain, which is 1120km (696 miles) to the northeast. Lanzarote lies on latitude 28° north, some 480km (298 miles) from the Tropic of Cancer. It is about 60km (37 miles) long and 21km (13 miles) wide at its broadest point, covering some 846km² (UNESCO data), 314 sq. miles. In addition to Lanzarote, there are six other islands in the archipelago – Tenerife, Gran Canaria, La Palma, Fuerteventura, La Gomera and El Hierro – as well as numerous islets, most of which are uninhabited. Together the Canary Islands cover about 7500km² (2895 square miles). They belong

▼ *Below: The Femés valley in the south of the island is noted for its vineyards.*

geographically to **Macronesia**, a group of islands (including Madeira and the Azores) of similar volcanic origin, topography and indigenous flora and fauna. The Canary Islands are about 40 million years old and were formed during the Tertiary geological era (around the same time as the Atlas Mountains in north Africa) as the African tectonic plate moved northeast and created a weakness in the earth's crust through which volcanic material poured. The Canary Islands can best be thought of as the tips of underwater volcanoes. There is also a theory that the two most easterly islands – Lanzarote and Fuerteventura – were once part of the African continent, although there is little proof of this. More evidence suggests that Lanzarote was once connected to Fuerteventura and the islands were separated due to the rise in sea level that followed the Ice Age.

The Volcanic History of Lanzarote

The first volcanic eruptions on Lanzarote occurred between 17 and 20 million years ago and they have continued until recently. Well-documented eruptions took place in the Timanfaya area between 1730 and 1736, when the lava and ash covered around two-thirds of the island and buried many villages and fertile agricultural land in the process. It appears

▲ *Above: A series of spectacular volcanoes in Timanfaya National Park.*

THE NAME 'CANARY'

There has always been controversy about the origins of the name 'Canary'. There are wild canaries in many parts of the archipelago (although not on Lanzarote), but these birds were probably named after the islands. A popular theory is that early settlers were impressed by the size of the dogs on the islands and used the Latin name for dogs (*canis*) to name the area. A further supposition is that the primitive inhabitants of the islands were Berbers from the Canarii tribe in Morocco.

that over 30 volcanoes were spewing out material at this time. A century later, in 1824, there was a further eruption in the same area, but it only lasted for two months. Since then, the volcanoes of Lanzarote have been dormant, but heat remains close to the surface and new eruptions could occur at any time. It is a relief to know that scientists monitor these volcanoes and are able to predict an eruption as long as a week in advance.

Mountains and Rivers

The landscape of Lanzarote has been shaped by its volcanic activity, which has left two main volcanic massifs, Famara-Guatifay in the north and Los Ajaches in the south. Lanzarote's highest mountain, volcano **Peñas del Chache**, rises to 670m (2198ft) and can be seen between the towns of Haría and Los Valles. Further north is **Mount Corona**, rising 609m (1998ft), the eruptions of which led to a huge spread of lava, leaving a wide area of *malpaís* or badlands (the terms apply to a recent lava flow that has not matured sufficiently for a soil to develop for agricultural use). Within the lava are numerous caves or **volcanic tubes** (part of the Atlantic Tube System), such as the **Jameos del Agua** and the **Cueva de los Verdes**, which are among the most popular tourist attractions on the island. The massif of Los Ajaches in the south is less dramatic, but it is a fine display of black basalt lava.

The most recent volcanic activity occurred in the south-west of Lanzarote in an area known as **Timanfaya**. This area has been a **national park** since 1974. Nearly three-quarters of the park is covered with lava or ash and is devoid of plant life except for occasional spreads of lichens. The park has a number of volcanoes over 500m (1650ft) in height, known as the **Montañas del Fuego** (Mountains of Fire), and many other superb volcanic features. Some of the volcanoes have deep craters, such as that on the **Caldera de Corazoncillo**, which is 33m (108ft) deep. In other parts of the park there are small cones, known as *hornitos* (little ovens), formed by exploding gas. The volcanic landscape is extremely colourful, with shades of red, yellow and brown.

Between the volcanic massifs are plains of volcanic ash, gravel and *picón* (small, black, porous volcanic pebbles used in agriculture as a substitute soil), such as **El Rubicón** in the south of the island and **El Jable** in the centre. Surprisingly, these areas are not entirely devoid of fertility, as the *picón* is able to retain sufficient moisture to support vines and other crops.

Lanzarote has no permanently flowing rivers, owing to its low rainfall. There are many ***barrancos*** (valleys) that have temporary streams during the winter, but the majority of valleys on the island are dry. These *barrancos* were probably formed during the wetter climatic times immediately after the Ice Age.

The Legend of Atlantis

The legend of the lost continent of Atlantis is a persistent theme in Greek and Roman mythology. The idea was that a large continent, called Atlantis, lay somewhere to the west of Gibraltar. It was thought to be a sort of Utopia, but it had almost entirely slipped under the waves and disappeared. Plato, basing his evidence on the stories of mariners, claimed that only seven mountain tops remained above the waves. Is it a coincidence that the seven main islands of the Canaries all have volcanic peaks?

Seas and Shores

The deep waters of the **Atlantic Ocean** surround Lanzarote and their erosive power has shaped and produced the island's varied coastline. The most spectacular **cliffs**, known as the **Risco de Famara**, are found on the northwest tip of the island. They rise to over 500m (1640ft) and have a number of *miradors* (viewpoints) that provide spectacular views of Isla Graciosa. There are some impressive *puntas* (headlands) where the basalt lava reaches the sea, such as Punta Fariones in the north of the island and Punta de

◀ *Left: The resort of Playa Blanca is backed by a red volcanic cone.*

INTRODUCING LANZAROTE

Pechiguera – with its prominent lighthouse – in the south. In between the headlands are sandy beaches, some with black volcanic sand and others, like those at **Papagayo**, with golden sand. Some extraordinary features are the result of volcanoes found on the coast itself and a spectacular example is **El Golfo** in the southwest of Lanzarote. Here the sea has breached a volcanic cone and flooded the crater, creating a bright green lagoon, which is a popular tourist attraction.

The coast is also the site of a number of commercial *salinas* (salt pans), such as **Salinas del Río** in the north and **Salinas de Janubio** in the southwest. The salinas produced salt for the preservation of fish, but today modern cooling plants have replaced this method of salt production. Tourists can still view the salt pans and they provide significant ecological sites on the island as well as important stopovers for migrating birds.

Although the Atlantic Ocean is tidal, the lack of permanent rivers on Lanzarote means that there are no tidal estuaries, except for **Charco de San Ginés** – a sea-water lagoon situated right at the heart of the island's capital, Arrecife.

There are a few sand dunes on Isla Graciosa and neighbouring Fuerteventura, yet these are not typical features on the coastline of Lanzarote.

▶▶ *Opposite: The bird of paradise flower, or strelitzia, is common in hotel gardens.*
▶ *Right: Commercial salt pans at Salinas de Janubio in the south of the island.*

Climate

The climate of Lanzarote, along with that of the other Canary Islands, has been described as that of perpetual spring or eternal summer. Unlike the larger islands, such as Tenerife and Gran Canaria, there are no high mountains on Lanzarote, which results in moderate weather patterns on the island. The north of the island, however, is certainly windier than the rest of Lanzarote. The moist **trade winds** blow generally from the north, so that the windward northern coast has a little more rain and cloud than the leeward south, which is somewhat drier and hotter. The differences, however, are not great. The south of the island may enjoy as much as 2500 hours of **sunshine** annually, with temperatures varying from 18° to 24°C (64° to 75°F) in the summer and from 16° to 20°C (61° to 68°F) in the winter, although afternoon temperatures in both winter and summer can be considerably higher. Occasionally during the summer the hot sirocco wind blows from the Sahara bringing desert dust, high temperatures and discomfort to all. Locals refer to this phenomenon as *Tiempo Africano* (African Weather). **Rainfall** is generally light, averaging 117.5mm (4.6in), with the wettest months being January and October. Farmers rely on the nightly fall of dew to aid cultivation. The cool **Canary current** flows from the north and ensures that the sea temperatures around the island are lower than what might be expected at this latitude – being around 18°C (64°F) in the winter and rising to 22°C (72°F) in the summer.

Significantly, the weather makes Lanzarote an ideal all-year-round tourist destination, which is an important factor in the island's economy.

THE BIRD OF PARADISE FLOWER

Although many parts of Lanzarote are barren and infertile, gardens, parks and the environs of hotels are bright with exotic flowers and shrubs that have been brought to the island from many parts of the world. The favourite of most visitors is the **bird of paradise flower** (strelitzia). From glossy dark leaves, flower heads of orange, purple and blue protrude, resembling a crane's head in shape. The flowers make an ideal bedding plant on the island. If you fancy taking a strelitzia home, don't bother to take a cutting, as you can buy them at airport shops, already potted and packed for the journey.

INTRODUCING LANZAROTE

▲ *Above: Palms and bougainvilleas are among the exotic species growing in parks and gardens.*

JOINED TO AFRICA?

A theory suggests that Lanzarote was once joined to Africa. Supporters say that the sand on the island is similar to that of the Sahara, and fossilized eggs of the flightless elephant bird, which was once found on Africa, have been found here. Those who disagree say the sand could have blown over in the sirocco wind, while the eggs might have been brought in by man or be those of a flying bird.

Flora

The lack of varying altitudes, the recent spread of volcanic material and the arid climate on Lanzarote do not provide an environment for a large range of plant life, such as that on the western islands of the archipelago, to thrive. The plants that are found, however, are of great interest to botanists. Many plants are **indigenous** to the Canary Islands or to a single island. On the lava flows (*malpaís* or badlands), the first plants to grow are mosses (*Bryophyta*) and lichens, while the Canary houseleek (*Aeonuim canariense*) is often the first to appear in cracks and fissures. In the more humid parts of the world, the colonization of volcanic material can be rapid, but on arid Lanzarote the process has taken centuries.

Because of its aridity, **trees** are scarce on Lanzarote. A notable exception is in the Haría valley, where hundreds of Canary palms (*Phoenix canariensis*) are found. A few examples of the dragon tree (*Dracaena draco*) may be seen, although these were probably brought from the surrounding islands. The dragon tree, which survives for hundreds of years, is typical of the Canary Islands and was regarded with reverence by the Guanches who were the original inhabitants of the area.

Most of the wild plants seen on Lanzarote are **xerophious**, which means that they have adapted to thrive in dry conditions. Especially common on the scrubland areas are the **spurges** (*euphorbiaceae*) – plants that produce a bitter, milky juice. Growing widely is the candelabra spurge (*Euphorbia canariensis*), which looks like a cactus, and the wild spurge (*Euphorbia obtusifolia*), which has greenish yellow flowers. Near the coast of Lanzarote, the drought-resistant plants are also **halophytic** (salt-tolerant). These plants include seaside plantain (*Plantago aschersonii*), Canary sea lavender (*Limonium tuberculatum*) and sea grape (*Zigophyllum fontanesii*).

Public parks, gardens and the grounds of hotels are bright with **introduced plants**. After the Spanish Conquest, sailors and travellers brought in exotic flowers and shrubs from all over the world. They include bougainvilleas, hibiscuses, geraniums and strelitzias, as well as small trees such as mimosa and jacaranda. All flourish in Lanzarote and many hotel grounds resemble botanical gardens.

Fauna

The amount of animal life on Lanzarote is even less than the variety of flora. With the exception of bats, there is only one indigenous **mammal** on the island, a shrew (*Crocidura canariensis*) which is also found on neighbouring Fuerteventura. There are, however, a number of species that have been introduced to the island, such as the rabbit brought in by the Spaniards in the 14th century, but these are becoming increasingly rare. House mice, hedgehogs and black and brown rats have also settled on the island, and another introduced mammal that almost every visitor will see is the camel. Although they are called *camellos* on the island, they have only one hump and are actually dromedaries. They were introduced from north Africa to assist in agriculture, but are now mainly used to transport tourists around the Timanfaya National

▼ *Below: Plants are commonly grown in volcanic pebbles or picón.*

INTRODUCING LANZAROTE

Park. There are numerous **marine mammals** in the waters around Lanzarote and they include several species of whale, porpoise and dolphin. Whale-watching is becoming a popular tourist activity in many parts of the Canary Islands. Monk seals once bred on Isla de los Lobos, between Lanzarote and Fuerteventura, but they have been hunted to extinction. There are over 400 species of **fish** in the Atlantic around the Canary Islands and the stretch of water between Lanzarote and the African coast is a rich fishing ground, with good catches of *cherne* (stone bass), *sama* (red sea bream), *corvina* (sea bass) and *vieja* (parrot fish) – many of which are on menus at restaurants. Common shellfish include lobsters, prawns and mussels, and there are also game fish such as marlin, tuna, shark and swordfish.

There is a small, but interesting set of **birds** in the Canary Islands; only 47 species of birds have been recorded as breeding, and many of these are only spasmodic breeders or in danger of becoming extinct. Lanzarote itself has approximately 30 resident species, so visiting bird-watchers should time their visit to coincide with the spring migration.

Of particular interest are the desert species, which include the cream-coloured courser, the Houbara bustard, the trumpeter bullfinch and the Barbary partridge, but they are all difficult to spot. Common birds are the Berthalot's pipit, the great grey shrike (often seen on telephone wires), the spectacled warbler, the chiffchaff, the linnet, the raven and gulls. Day trippers to Arrecife should look out for the numerous pairs of cattle egrets that nest in the pine trees on the seafront. Ironically, the wild canary is not found on Lanzarote as it is a woodland bird.

Spring in Lanzarote is a good time to see a beautiful collection of **butterflies**, as many of these colourful creatures spend the summer in Europe, but actually breed in the Canary Islands before migrating. Included in this assortment are the

▲ *Above: The waters around Lanzarote are rich in fish life.*
◀ *Opposite: The raven, distinguished by its croaking call, is Lanzarote's largest bird.*

painted lady, speckled wood, clouded yellow, common blue, cleopatra and migrating monarchs. A moth that is worthy to be mentioned is the silver Y, which is known to migrate north alongside the painted ladies. Common **insects** include the unwelcome mosquito (although not the malaria-carrying type) and dragonflies, including the common red darter.

The **amphibians** and **reptiles** found on the island include lizards, geckoes and skinks. Geckoes are often found in houses and even in hotel bedrooms, where they effectively take care of the insects and are regarded by the locals as a sign of good luck. Thankfully there are no snakes in the Canary Islands! Three species of turtles can be seen in Canarian waters – the leatherback, loggerhead and green. None of them breed here, and they are all threatened species.

HISTORY IN BRIEF

The early history of the Canary Islands is shrouded in myth and mystery. The Greeks and Romans certainly knew of the islands' existence: Plato thought that they were the remains of the lost continent of Atlantis, while the geographer Ptolemy accurately located their position in AD150. It is highly unlikely, however, that either the Greeks or the Romans ever set foot on the Canary Islands. On the other hand the Phoenicians and the Carthaginians most certainly did.

THE BUTCHER BIRD

One interesting bird among the rather small avian population of Lanzarote is the **great grey shrike** (*Lanius excubitor*) – a handsome black, grey and white bird the size of a blackbird. It spends much of its time on a perch or a telephone wire waving its tail from side to side, searchimg for prey. It can be seen throughout the island, but particularly on farmland, where it catches small birds, mice, lizards and insects. Its habit of impaling its prey on thorns or barbed wire has led to its nickname – the butcher bird.

INTRODUCING LANZAROTE

▲ *Above: Souvenir shops and restaurants with terraces line the promenade at Playa Blanca.*

GUANCHE SKILLS

Although the Guanches, the original inhabitants of the Canary Islands, lived a Stone-Age existence and had no knowledge of the wheel or boat-building, they did have certain unusual skills. Thor Heyerdahl, the Norwegian explorer and anthropologist, claimed that they built **pyramids**. It is also known that they **mummified their dead**, particularly those in the higher echelons of society. Collections of skulls in various museums show that they also drilled holes in their heads – a medical process known as 'trepanning'. Anthropologists believe that the possession of these skills means that they originated in North Africa, probably as far east as Egypt.

Early Inhabitants

Remains of **Cro-Magnon Man** have been found in the Canary Islands. Examples of skulls with broad faces and high foreheads have been carbon dated to around 3000BC. When the Europeans explored the islands in the 14th century, they found a primitive people living there who were tall, blond and blue-eyed. The Tenerife name, the **Guanches**, has been adopted to describe the indigenous people of all the Canary Islands. Nobody is really certain of the origins of the Guanches (although most experts now believe that they were Berbers from North Africa) or how they got to the islands, as they appear to have had no knowledge of boat-building.

Guanche Society

The Europeans explored the islands and found a primitive, Stone-Age community with no knowledge of metals, the wheel, the building of boats or the bow and arrow. The majority lived in caves, which were easily carved out of the soft volcanic ash, although those of higher status lived in simple stone houses that were oval in shape. The Guanche economy was based on animal rearing and the growing of grain crops. The women made pots that were elaborately decorated and used the coil method rather than the wheel. Their clothing was made from sheep- and goatskins, and these animals provided them with meat, cheese and milk. The Guanches also ate fish, fruit and *gofio*, which was a sort of dumpling made from roasted grain flour (*see* panel, page 26).

Despite their primitive way of life, the Guanches had a sophisticated social structure. Their society was divided into castes and they were ruled by an elected king. They worshipped the sun, believed in life after death, and their *faycans* (priests) were regarded as important people. Women played a significant role in society and they could become kings or *faycans*. There was no death penalty, but murderers were severely beaten and their possessions were given to the relatives of their victims as compensation. They also mummified their dead from the highest social strata, using skins and reeds before laying them in burial caves. It is believed that a single Guanche language was spoken (although not written) throughout the islands, with possible local dialects. This suggests that the Guanches had a common origin, since there was very little communication between the various islands.

The Arrival of Europeans

Around 1312, a Genoese navigator named **Lancelotto Malocello** landed on Lanzarote and it is believed that he was responsible for the island's name. He lived on the island for some time before being killed by the Guanches. At this stage the island was familiar to Europeans, and the Portuguese and Spaniards invaded it on numerous occasions and took many of the natives away to be slaves.

VERDINO DOGS

It is often claimed that the Canary Islands gained their name from the Latin word *canus*, which means dog. Historical records often mention the large dogs that were found on the islands, and some research suggests that the inhabitants actually ate the dogs. The Spanish Conquistadors were rather scared of these dogs and eventually passed a law to ensure that they be put down, but allowed each shepherd one dog to guard his flocks. Known as **verdinos**, because of the slightly green tinge to their coats, the dogs were smooth-haired with broad jaws. They were noted for their ferocity, but also for their loyalty to their owners. Today there is an organization which aims to keep the verdino strain pure and have it registered as a breed.

◄ *Left: A kid at a farm above Femés. Goats are the most common domestic animals on Lanzarote.*

INTRODUCING LANZAROTE

POLICEMEN

Hopefully, visitors to Lanzarote will not need to contact a policeman – which is just as well, because, confusingly, there are three different Spanish police forces. Firstly, there are the **Policia Municipal**, who wear blue uniforms and carry out minor duties such as traffic control. There are also the **Policia Nacional**, who have brown uniforms and deal with burglaries and robberies. Finally, there are the **Guardia Civil**, who wear light green uniforms. They were once greatly feared, but now the Guardia Civil have a less important role and spend much of their time on motorcycles doing traffic duty. All Spanish policemen and women are armed and not especially noted for their sense of humour. Don't adopt a frivolous approach towards them!

The French Connection

A major development in the history of Lanzarote came about in 1402 when two Frenchmen, **Gadifer de la Salle** and **Jean de Béthencourt,** led a small military expedition to Lanzarote. The whole exploit was something of a fiasco as two-thirds of the men deserted in Cadiz, which left around 60 men to land in the north of the island. The Guanche leader, who thought that the French party would protect the islanders from further slave raids, greeted them. De Béthencourt then left for Europe to offer the sovereignty of Lanzarote to whichever court could give him the highest reward. De la Salle, in the meantime, was having trouble with the Guanches and it took a full-scale war before they were finally defeated in 1404. The leader of the Guanches, Guardafía, was baptized along with many of his followers. De Béthencourt, who had been made King of Lanzarote by the Spanish court, returned to the island and succeeded de la Salle. He then recruited a number of *Lanzaroteños* and set out to conquer the rest of the Canary Islands. He swiftly overcame Fuerteventura, El Hierro and La Gomera, and left his nephew, Maciot, in charge while returning to France. Maciot married the daughter of the Guanche leader and set up his headquarters at Teguise. Within the next few years the first churches were built on the island.

The Spanish Conquest

The capture of Lanzarote, Fuerteventura and La Gomera was, in fact, no great feat, because the small Guanche population on these islands had been decimated by diseases that were introduced by the Europeans during the years of slave trading. The larger and more populated islands of Gran Canaria and Tenerife offered a more determined resistance.

Spain began the second phase of the Conquest in 1478, when Ferdinand and Isabella, *Los Reyes Católicos* (the Catholic monarchs), sanctioned an attack on Gran Canaria. The Spanish forces met fierce resistance from the Guanches and the turning point came when a new military governor, **Pedro de Vera**, arrived in 1480. He applied

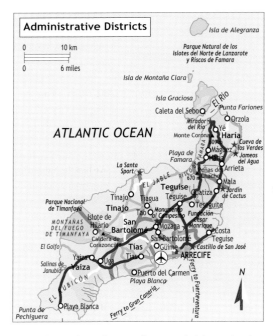

Administrative Districts

Isla de Alegranza

0   10 km

0   6 miles

Parque Natural de los
Islotes del Norte de Lanzarote
y Riscos de Famara

Isla de Montaña Clara

ATLANTIC OCEAN

Isla Graciosa

Caleta del Sebo — Punta Fariones

Mirador
del Río — Yé — Orzola

Monte Corona — Haria — Cueva de
los Verdes

Máguez — Jameos
del Agua

Playa de
Famara — Arrieta

La Santa
Sport — Peñas del
Chache — Mala

670 m — Jardin
de Cactus

Teguise — Guatiza

Tinajo — Tiagua — Teguise — Teseguite

Parque Nacional
de Timanfaya — **Tinajo** — Tao — Monumento
al Campesino — Fundación
César
Manrique

MONTAÑAS
DEL FUEGO — Islote de
Hilario — **San
Bartolomé** — Mozaga — Costa
Teguise

DE TIMANFAYA — Caldera de
Corazoncillo — San Bartolomé

El Golfo — **Tías** — Güime — Castillo de San José

Yaiza — Tías — **ARRECIFE**

Salinas de
Janubio — **Yaiza** — Uga

EL RUBICÓN — Puerto del Carmen

Playa Blanca

Punta de
Pechiguera — Playa Blanca

Ferry to Gran Canaria

Ferry to Fuerteventura

N

aggressive tactics and eventually persuaded the two local
Guanche kings to convert to Christianity. Nevertheless, it
was 1483 before Gran Canaria was completely defeated.

The next Spanish commander on the scene was **Alonso
Fernández de Lugo**, who in 1491 received royal assent to
attack La Palma and Tenerife. La Palma was quickly taken,
but Tenerife was to prove the toughest island to overcome.
De Lugo arrived on the island in 1493 with a force of 1000
soldiers plus Guanche mercenaries from other islands. There
were a number of battles and de Lugo had to send for extra
men from Spain before Tenerife was finally overcome.

Post-Conquest Guanches

After the Conquest, the various islands were administered
for Spain by *capitanes-generales*. Many Guanches died
from European diseases to which they had no resistance,
and a large number of them were taken to Spain as slaves

(although many were allowed to return). Others assumed Spanish names and were converted to Christianity. Assimilation with the colonists came swiftly and the Guanches' spoken language quickly disappeared. Despite this, modern anthropological research claims that several of Guanche characteristics are evident in the everyday life on the Canary Islands. Certainly a great number of the inhabitants of the Canary Islands are very proud of their Guanche ancestry, as they feel that this highlights the difference between themselves and mainland Spaniards.

▲ Above: Vines growing in volcanic gravel sheltered by stone walls.

SUCCESSFUL INTRODUCTIONS

With the exception of bats, there are no native **mammals** on Lanzarote. There have been several attempts to introduce some to the island. The **Algerian hedgehog** (*Atelerix algirus*) was introduced to Fuerteventura at the end of the 19th century and later spread to Lanzarote. The striped **ground squirrel** (*Atlantoxerus getulus*) has also been introduced to Fuerteventura. These animals live colonially in burrows in the ground and in some parts of the island they have become a pest.

Spanish Colonial Rule

For the next three or four centuries the Canary Islands experienced mixed fortunes under Spanish colonial rule. The islands attracted large numbers of settlers, not only from Spain, but also from Portugal, France and Italy. After Columbus's discovery of the New World in 1492, ports such as Las Palmas on Gran Canaria and Santa Cruz on Tenerife became important staging posts for ships travelling to and from the Americas. Lanzarote, with no suitable harbour, gained little from this transatlantic business. Since Lanzarote is the most easterly island in the archipelago, it also attracted more than its fair share of corsairs from countries opposed to Spain, such as Britain, Holland and Portugal, while pirates from the north coast of Africa were always a threat, sacking Teguise on numerous occasions.

Consequently, a number of fortresses were built, including Santa Bárbara near Teguise, the Castillo de San Gabriel to protect Arrecife, and the Tower of San Marcial del Rubicón in the south of the island. By the 19th century, invasions by buccaneers had become less of a problem and this allowed the island's capital to move from Teguise to the port of Arrecife in 1852.

Boom and Bust

During the years of Spanish colonial rule, the Canary Islands experienced turbulent economic fortunes. Reliance on various types of monoculture led to cycles of 'boom and bust' and mass emigrations to the New World. The first industry to collapse was that of **sugar cane**, due to the abolition of slavery and the cheaper sugar produced in central and southern America. Lanzarote was fortunate as it was never able to specialize in sugar cane because of its dry climate. Sugar was replaced by the production of **wine**. The wine boom, however, was over by the start of the 19th century, because of the competition from Madeira and diseases affecting the vines. This led to further emigration.

In 1825, a new product was discovered. This was **cochineal** (a red dye), which was extracted from a small parasitic insect found on cactus plants. Thousands of prickly pear cactus plants soon appeared on Lanzarote and this unusual type of farming boomed. By the 1870s chemical dyes began to appear on the market and the cochineal trade fell away, which resulted in yet more emigration. Strangely though, both wine and cochineal continue to be produced on Lanzarote, more so than on any of the other Canary Islands.

▼ *Below: Prickly pear. This succulent is a host plant for the cochineal beetle.*

INTRODUCING LANZAROTE

Political Developments

The Canary Islands were declared a province of Spain in 1821, with Santa Cruz de Tenerife as the capital. Rivalry between Tenerife and Gran Canaria was prevalent, with Tenerife proving to dominate, while Lanzarote – with its small population and lack of economic clout – gradually became something of a political backwater.

A measure of political independence was established in 1912 when Spain introduced island councils or *cabildos*. In 1927 the Spanish government divided the Canary Islands into two provinces. The Eastern Province included Lanzarote, Fuerteventura and Gran Canaria, with its capital at Las Palmas, while the Western Province was made up of Tenerife and the smaller islands of La Gomera, El Hierro and La Palma, with the capital at Santa Cruz de Tenerife.

The Canary Islands' economy showed an upturn during the late 19th and early 20th centuries. This was influenced by their designation as a **free trade zone** and the growth of the Atlantic steamship trade. In the 1850s, British entrepreneurs introduced banana and tomato farming to the islands, but unfortunately Lanzarote's arid climate was unsuitable for these crops. The disruption caused by two world wars led to unemployment and a further wave of emigration to the Americas. The extent of this emigration is illustrated by the fact that over a quarter of a million people

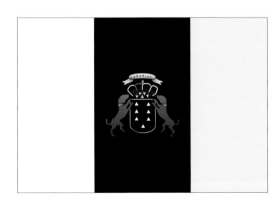

▶ *Right: The regional flag of the Canary Islands is flown on all public occasions.*

HISTORICAL CALENDAR

3000BC Archaeological evidence from skulls suggests that the Canary Islands were inhabited by Cro-Magnon Man.

1100BC Phoenicians and Carthaginians are believed to have visited the Canary Islands.

1312 Genoese explorer, Lancelotto Malocello, occupies and names Lanzarote.

1340 Portugal and Spain send ships to investigate the islands, finding Guanches living a Stone-Age existence.

1401 Spanish Conquest begins with an expedition led by Jean de Béthencourt, who soon conquers Lanzarote. He makes a treaty with the local Guanche king who welcomes protection from pirate raids. Lanzarote becomes a base for attacks on the other islands, using a number of Guanche mercenaries.

1483 Gran Canaria is finally subdued.

1492 Columbus makes his first visit to the Canary Islands and observes an eruption of Mount Teide on Tenerife.

1494 Tenerife is the last island to fall to the Spanish forces.

15th and 16th centuries The Spanish colonize the islands, with the settlers developing a thriving economy, aided by the slave trade. Navies and buccaneers of rival countries pose a constant threat.

1730–36 Volcanic eruptions on Lanzarote destroy many villages and large areas of farmland, leading to mass emigration to Latin America.

Early 18th century The cochineal industry reaches its peak on Lanzarote.

1852 Isabella II declares the Canaries a Free Trade Zone.

1927 Canaries divided into two zones, with Las Palmas as capital of the Eastern Province, consisting of Gran Canaria, Lanzarote and Fuerteventura.

1936 General Franco plots a military coup, leading to the Spanish Civil War. Lanzarote is affected by the closure of the trade routes.

1970s Tourism begins to take off in Lanzarote.

1982 Regional Constitution granted by Spain to the Canary Islands.

1986 Canary Islands granted special status within the European Union.

2002 Introduction of the Euro.

2014 Spanish oil company Repsol begins exploration in the waters of the Canary Islands despite local protests.

of Canary Island origin are estimated to live in Caracas, the capital of Venezuela. The full story of the history of emigration can be seen in the Museum of the Emigrant in Castillo de Santa Bárbara, just outside the old capital of Teguise. In the 19th century, Lanzarote's population was reduced by over a third, but it stabilized during the 20th century after the discovery of the *enarenado* system of agriculture, which uses volcanic clinker to preserve water.

The Rise of Franco

In the 1930s the Canary Islands found themselves to be involved in the Spanish Civil War. In March 1936, General Franco, who was suspected of planning a coup to overthrow the government, was exiled to Tenerife with the post of *Comandante-General*. Franco was in the Canary Islands for a mere four months, but during this time he survived no fewer than three assassination attempts. He eventually went to

INTRODUCING LANZAROTE

▶ *Right: The attractive town hall in San Bartolomé in central Lanzarote.*

Morocco to lead the insurgents, and began the brutal Civil War that was to divide towns and families throughout Spain.

The Growth of Tourism

Franco largely ignored the Canary Islands while he was in power in Spain, giving rise to an active separatist movement in the archipelago. The movement was only stemmed in 1982, when the Canaries (and other parts of Spain) were given autonomous powers and a regional constitution. Another factor that quelled nationalism was the growth of **tourism**, which has provided considerable employment and is now Lanzarote's main source of convertible revenue. Indeed the number of tourists on the island often exceeds the number of indigenous inhabitants.

GOVERNMENT AND ECONOMY

Government

The two provinces of the Canary Islands form one of the 17 autonomous regional communities in Spain. Rivalry between the islands is part of their history and the regional government has offices in both Santa Cruz de Tenerife and Las Palmas on Gran Canaria. The regional government has powers covering transport, agriculture, health and policing,

THE RABBIT HUNTERS

It is a common habit in Spain to give the inhabitants of towns or regions certain names that are related to their past way of life. The people of Lanzarote, for example, are known as **conejeros**, which is translated as rabbit hunters. But where are these rabbits on the island? Few visitors will ever see these animals in the wild (there are very few to be hunted for food) and if rabbit is offered on a restaurant's menu, it will probably have been reared domestically. It is possible, of course, that rabbits once thrived on Lanzarote and were wiped out by the 18th-century volcanic eruptions.

and it also has the ability to raise local taxes. Each island has its own local administration known as the *cabildo*, while a further level of adminstration is the district or *municipio*. Lanzarote is divided into seven administrative districts – Haría, Teguise, Arrecife, Tinajo, San Bartolomé, Tías and Yaiza (*see* map, page 19) – so that burgeoning holiday resorts can be administered conveniently.

The main **political parties** are the left-wing Partido Socialista Obrero Español (PSOE) and the right-of-centre Partido Popular (PP). In the 1990s various nationalist groups merged to form the Coalición Canaria (CC), which now – rather than pressing for independence – pushes Madrid for improvements. Most recent governments have been coalitions between the various parties.

The Economy

Canarian **agriculture** has diversified over the years, as farmers have learnt that farming a single product is not profitable in the long run, and now most farms have a variety of enterprises. The number of crops that can be grown on Lanzarote is somewhat restricted by the dry climate and lack of irrigation, especially in comparison to the larger and more mountainous islands to the west. Onions, tomatoes and potatoes are the major crops and all of these are grown in abundance. Wine from the *malvasía* grape is exported, mainly to the other Canary Islands. Other crops include various types of legumes, melons and tobacco. The basis of all crop farming on Lanzarote is the *enarenado* method, whereby plants are grown in black volcanic gravel or *picón*, which has the ability to absorb dew and prevent evaporation. Livestock is rare on Lanzarote and visitors to the island are unlikely to see any cattle or sheep. Goats and donkeys are kept and the occasional camel is still seen working in the fields.

The other traditional mainstay of the Lanzarote economy is **fishing**. There are rich fishing grounds between the east of the island and the African coast, and Arrecife has the largest fishing fleet in the Canary Islands. Large numbers of sardines, sea bass, *vieja* and cod are caught here. Associated industries

GOAT'S-MILK CHEESE

Although there are no cattle kept on Lanzarote (as there is no grass to feed them), there are over 8000 goats. Formerly farmed for their milk, they are now largely used for cheese production. The cheese varies in appearance – it can be yellow and hard or white and crumbly. Generally speaking, the darker the colour, the better it keeps. One interesting variety is called *ahumado*, which is smoked over prickly pear leaves. Lanzarote goat's-milk cheese is on sale in all supermarkets, and all self-catering visitors should certainly try some.

GOFIO

This is one of the few culinary items to have survived since Guanche times. *Gofio* was once made from the glasswort plant, but after the Spanish introduced Indian maize, this became the main ingredient. It is mixed with wheat flour and toasted (or roasted). It is then used in a variety of ways: it can be sprinkled on food, used to thicken stews or soups, made into a breakfast food, or mixed with figs or almonds to make a dessert. Unfortunately, few visitors to Lanzarote get the opportunity to try *gofio*, as it is rarely on the menu in the main tourist resorts. Those who are keen to try this Canarian food need to drive into the interior of the island in order to find a rural restaurant that has *gofio* on the menu.

include canning and the production of fish bone meal. Vast numbers of fish can be seen in the clear waters of Lanzarote's harbours, and a popular habit of tourists is to throw bread to the fish – the waters seem to boil with fish desperate for a bite.

In recent years there has been a startling growth in **tourism**. The Canary Islands are an all-year-round destination attracting over 10 million visitors annually, mainly from Britain, Germany, Scandinavia, Holland and mainland Spain. Of this total, Lanzarote attracts around 2 million tourists annually. Tourism also provides a vast number of jobs in the construction industry, which has been booming over the last decade. It is estimated that over 90 per cent of the working population of Lanzarote is involved with tourism in some way. The income from tourism has had the effect of improving the island's infrastructure to the benefit of *Lanzaroteños* and visitors alike. Nevertheless, across the Canary Islands 33% of the population is unemployed, with the bulk being young people (although there is a sizeable grey economy) and average wages are among the lowest in the EU.

▶ *Right: Women in local costume at a* feria *at Teguise.*

THE PEOPLE

The total **population** of the Canary Islands currently stands at 2,117,519 and grows at a rate of more than 1 per cent annually. The last census found that Lanzarote has 141,437 inhabitants, about a third of whom live in the capital, Arrecife. These totals include a good number of foreign residents, mainly from Britain and Germany. There are also small numbers from Latin America, largely made up of returning emigrants from such countries as Cuba and Venezuela. The people of Lanzarote are mainly descendants of Spaniards and they are generally dark haired and have an olive complexion. They are fiercely patriotic and regard themselves as *Canarios*, rather than from the 'peninsula', which is their name for mainland Spain. They have mixed feelings towards mainland Spaniards, call them *godos* (or Goths) and accuse them of taking local jobs. Indeed, many *Canarios* like to think of themselves as African rather than Spanish. Employers, however, often prefer to offer jobs to the mainland Spaniards, whom they regard as more reliable.

Like mainland Spaniards, *Canarios* are family-orientated. Machismo is still prevalent, but women have become increasingly liberated and now play a large role in public life, with many employed in the tourist industry.

Religion

The Spanish invaders brought **Roman Catholicism** with them to the Canary Islands and they swiftly converted the Guanches. It is still the official religion and it plays an important part in the lives of the people. Although weekly church attendance is not very high, most *Canarios* have church baptisms, weddings and funerals and attend church for various religious events noted on their calendar.

Festivals

Fiestas are the traditional way of celebrating Saints' days on the religious calendar. These include Easter (*Semana Santa*); *Corpus Christi*, when floral carpets are laid out on the streets; and the *Fiestas del Carmen*, marked by processions of boats.

CHILD-FRIENDLY ISLAND

Do not worry about taking babies or young children to Lanzarote, as they are made very welcome. Local children keep very late nights and are not excluded from any family activities. Waiters traditionally make a huge fuss of small children who come to their restaurants and prepare special portions for them. Older children will find plenty to occupy themselves, from sandy beaches to theme parks and boat trips.

INTRODUCING LANZAROTE

▶ *Right: The simple lines of the whitewashed church at Playa Blanca.*

Romerías are processions led by decorated ox carts, which head from town churches to a hermitage (a place where a revered image is kept) or similar location. There are many festivals of a secular nature and these may include a week-long *feria* (fair). Fiestas on Lanzarote are usually accompanied by colourful fireworks, bonfires, parades, wrestling matches and traditional folk dancing and singing.

THE CEREMONY OF THE DYING SARDINE

Many of the coastal fiestas in the Canary Islands end with a curious ceremony involving a giant mock-up of a sardine. It is often 'rescued' from the beach and taken to a shopping centre by an entourage of doctors and nurses. An emergency operation is carried out in an 'operating theatre', but the sardine always dies. There is a funeral procession through the streets and its last will and testament is read out by a famous personality. The giant sardine is finally cremated on a huge bonfire. The fireworks then begin and this marks the end of the fiesta.

Sport and Recreation

The Canary Islands have some unique forms of sports that go back centuries and are enthusiastically followed by the locals. *Lucha Canaria* (Canarian wrestling) had its origins in Guanche trials of strength. Bullfighting is not popular in the Canary Islands, but sand-covered arenas resembling bull-rings are used for wrestling competitions. Each village has its own wrestling team and *luchas* (competitions) are often held at original Guanche locations during fiestas. *Juego del Palo* (stick fighting) also originated in pre-Conquest days. It is a contest using 2m (6.6ft) wooden staves called *banot* with which contestants aim to do maximum damage to each other. Even longer staves of around 2.5m (8.2ft) are used in the *El Salto del Pastor*, a form of pole vaulting in which contestants leap down a mountainside and across deep ravines. Less appealing to tourists is **cock fighting**, which has a strong following in Lanzarote.

The more international spectator sports are also extremely popular in the Canary Islands. As in the rest of Spain, **football** is obsessively followed. UD Las Palmas are in the Spanish second division and their local matches against rival Club Deportivo Tenerife are among the highlights of the Canary Islands' sporting year. There are plenty of activities available for visitors to Lanzarote and it is possible to base a holiday around sport by staying at **Club la Santa** near Tinajo, in the northwest of the island, and rub shoulders with world-famous sportsmen and women. Lanzarote now has two 18-hole **golf** courses, one at Costa Teguise and the other at Puerto del Carmen, and most of the large hotels offer **tennis** and **swimming** facilities. The Atlantic Ocean offers many possibilities for **water sports**. **Surfing** (particularly on the north coast), **sailing**, **windsurfing** and **power-boat racing** are all highly popular. The clear and warm waters of the Atlantic are perfect for **scuba diving** and **snorkelling**, and there are a number of undersea natural parks around the shores of the islands. The ocean also provides ideal conditions for **game fishing**. Charter boats are available for swordfish, tuna, shark and marlin fishing. Other recreational activities on offer in Lanzarote include **cycling** (bikes can be hired at most resorts), **horse riding** (there are a number of equestrian centres where horses may be hired) and **karting**.

Food and Drink

The **food** of Lanzarote illustrates a wide range of influences from other countries, including mainland Spain, northern Europe and even the Americas. Typical Canarian food is most likely to be found in the capital, Arrecife, and the inland towns and villages, rather than in the main resorts, where restaurants tend to serve international food with a Spanish flavour. If the visitor wishes to sample true Canarian food then the unusual meal times must be appreciated. **Breakfast**

Although there are no cathedrals on Lanzarote, there is an interesting selection of churches to visit. Many churches date from the early 16th century and display a variety of styles. Few are genuinely **Gothic** as this style was on the way out when the Spaniards were colonizing the islands, but there are many examples of the *Mudéjar* style, which had its origins in the Moorish occupation of southern Spain. Other churches display the ornate *Plateresque* decoration named after the work of silversmiths. Look out for some marvellously carved wooden ceilings. Stained-glass windows are generally uninspiring, but this is more than compensated for by the superb decorating of interiors. The altar screens (*retablos*) are often elaborately carved and dripping with gold leaf. Many churches have carvings by Luján Pérez (1756–1815), the greatest of Canarian sculptors. When visiting Lanzarote's churches, remember that beachwear is inappropriate and not appreciated by the locals.

INTRODUCING LANZAROTE

Spanish-style Snacks

Tapas are believed to have originated in Sevilla during the 19th century, when drinkers protected their glasses of *fino* from dust, flies and dripping hams by putting a *tapa* (cover) over their glass. The cover was often a slice of bread on which enterprising bartenders began to add food. The rest, as they say, is history. Spain's quirky meal times encourage taking the occasional snack to fill the gap. The days when a free *tapa* was provided with a drink are largely over, but a *tapas* crawl is one of the delights that the Canary Islands have to offer. *Tapas* vary from a simple dish of olives, or a slice of cheese, to quite sophisticated dishes. Remember, it is cheaper to take your *tapas* standing at a bar than sitting at a table.

(*desayuno*) is generally light and rarely served before 09:30. It usually consists of coffee, a sandwich (*bocadillo*) or a small cake (*pastel*). **Lunch** (*almuerzo*) is usually eaten after 14:30 and may have been preceded by tapas, which are light snacks served at the bar. Lunch, for many *Canarios*, is the main meal of the day and dinner (*cena*) is a lighter meal, which is usually eaten after 22:00. Hotels and restaurants in tourist areas will, of course, provide meals at times to suit visitors.

There are two fares in Lanzarote that the visitor should certainly sample. One is *gofio* (ground and toasted wheat or maize), the island's traditional staple food, which goes back to Guanche times. The other is *papas arrugadas*, small new potatoes with wrinkly skins, which are boiled in very salty water and served with most main courses.

Main meals in the resort restaurants of Lanzarote are usually introduced with a starter, such as a salad (*ensalada*) or a soup (*sopa*). Particular favourites are fish soup (*sopa de pescada*) and vegetable soup (*sopa de verdura*). Most restaurants also offer the popular mainland cold soup, *gazpacho*, which consists of finely chopped onions, tomatoes and garlic. The main course usually includes meat (*carne*) or fish (*pescado*). The most commonly offered meats are beef (*ternera*), chicken (*pollo*), lamb (*cordero*), pork (*cerdo*) and rabbit (*conejo*). The wild rabbits are hunted on the island or reared domestically for the table, but the other meat is imported. The meat may be grilled (*a la parilla*), roasted (*asado*) or it may be prepared in a stew (*estafado* or *puchero*).

A mouthwatering variety of **fish** and **shellfish** are also found on menus, with some significant differences to the selection found on Spain's Mediterranean coast. Fish is usually prepared simply, being fried (*frito*) or grilled (*a la plancha*). At some of the better fish restaurants, it is possible to choose your own fish from a tank or a display refrigerator, but the price is subject to the weight of the fish. The most common fish on the menu are sea bass (*cherne*), hake (*merluza*), swordfish (*pez espada*), sole (*lenguado*),

◄ *Left: Canarian lunch – lentil soup, Canarian fish, sauces and potatoes.*

tuna (*atun* or *bonito*) and parrotfish (*vieja*). Some excellent shellfish is also available, including prawns (*gambas*), mussels (*mejiones*) and squid (*calamares*). The traditional fish stew (*sancocho*) should be sought out. Particular Canarian specialities are the sauces that are provided with the fish and meat dishes. The red *mojo rojo* is a spicy vinaigrette-type sauce made from a mixture of chilli, cumin, paprika and saffron, and usually served with meat. *Mojo verde* is a green variation prepared with coriander or parsley instead of paprika, making a perfect accompaniment to fish. Vegetables are rather limited on Lanzarote and salad is usually served as a garnish to most main dishes.

The choice of **desserts** (*postres*) is usually confined to traditional Spanish favourites such as crème caramel (*flan*), ice cream (*helado*) or fruit (*fruta*). You might be lucky enough to be offered a traditional local dessert such as *frangollas* (a corn-based milk pudding flavoured with cinnamon, honey and brandy) or *torrijas* (sweet fritters of maize flour flavoured with honey and aniseed). Bananas are grown on neighbouring islands and they are a favourite dessert. They are often served fried with a topping of sugar, brandy and lemon juice. Any local cheese on offer will be goat's-milk cheese, or *queso blanca* (*see* panel, page 25), which is produced near Teguise.

The main resort areas in the south of Lanzarote also offer

THE UNUSUAL *TIMPLE*

On the island of Lanzarote, most traditional dancing and songs are accompanied by the *timple* (pronounced 'tim-play'). It is a stringed instrument, similar to the ukulele and the mandolin, made of wood and it has a rounded back. It normally has five strings, although there is a four-stringed version called the *contra* that is found on Lanzarote, but not on any of the other islands. Once thought to have originated from the Spanish *guitarillo*, it is now believed to have been brought to the islands by Berber slaves. The *timple* is played at local fiestas. It was even exported to Latin American countries with the many waves of emigrants, and it characterizes the folk music of both Cuba and Venezuela. On Lanzarote, the *timple* is traditionally made in the old capital of Teguise. The souvenir shops at Lanzarote airport sell CDs featuring *timple* music, and the instruments themselves are a fitting souvenir of a holiday on the island.

INTRODUCING LANZAROTE

▶ *Right: A chef descales fish for his restaurant on the beach at Playa Blanca.*

USEFUL WEBSITES

The following websites all contain useful information about Lanzarote:
www.lanzarote.com
www.discoverlanzarote.com
www.lanzaroteinformation.com
www.fuerteventura.com

CHURROS

Breakfast for most working *Lanzaroteños* is a hurried affair, often taken in a bar en route to work, rather than at home. Coffee and toast or a pastry probably satisfies most people, but the islanders have a sweet tooth and there are many devotees of *churros*. These are short sticks of a sort of deep-fried doughnut, which are dipped in a drink of hot chocolate. They are very fattening!

a bewildering variety of foreign restaurants. Chinese restaurants are particularly common, but many other nationalities are also represented. English breakfasts are offered in many places. Visitors on a budget should try the menu of the day (*menu del día*), which usually includes a starter, main course and a dessert, as well as bread and a drink, for a bargain price.

Sampling local **alcoholic drinks** is a pleasant part of many people's holiday, and Lanzarote offers plenty of choices at very reasonable prices. You will find **wine** from many parts of the world in the local supermarkets, but one must try the local *malvasía* wine, which is cultivated in the La Geria, San Bartolomé and Mozaga areas. Look particularly for the award-winning *El Grifo* wine – but beware, the *malvasías* can be 17 per cent proof and similar to a sherry in strength. Most wines served in restaurants, however, are from the Spanish mainland. There are some popular wine-based summer drinks, including *tinto de verano*, a mixture of red wine and lemonade, and the deceptively strong *sangria*, which is a combination of red wine, lemonade and liqueurs, garnished with fruit and ice. The most common **beers** are *Dorada*, which is made on

Tenerife, and *Tropical* from Gran Canaria. There are also beers from the Spanish mainland, such as *San Miguel* and *Cruz Campo*, as well as a host of foreign brews. For a small draught beer ask for *una caña*. The best-known Canarian spirit is rum (*ron*), which is made from locally grown sugar cane on Gran Canaria. The same factory also makes *ron miel*, a rum liqueur with added honey. There are a number of other **liqueurs** made from the subtropical fruits grown on the larger, wetter islands of the archipelago. The most popular is *cobana*, a yellow banana liqueur that comes in a striking bottle. Remember that spirit measures (if they are used at all) are two or three times larger than one would expect at home.

The most popular **non-alcoholic** drink is coffee, which comes in a variety of forms. Any bar with a good reputation will make its coffee in an espresso machine; for an espresso-type coffee, ask either for a *café solo* (which is black) or *café cortado* (which has just a drop of milk). *Café con leche* is milky coffee. Don't be surprised if your coffee arrives in a glass. *Canarios* often take a shot of rum in their coffee or have an accompanying *coñac*. Tea is also available, but usually served rather weak. A chocolate drink with breakfast is popular among *Lanzaroteños*, who often dunk their *churros* (a form of doughnut) into the beverage. A full range of soft drinks (*refrescos*) and fruit juices (*zumos*) are also available.

NIGHTLIFE

Compared with Tenerife and Gran Canaria, nightlife on Lanzarote is relatively subdued. This is definitely not 'lager lout' territory. Most entertainment takes place in the *Centros Comerciales*. Shopping centres by day, their bars and discos start livening up in the late evening and some may stay open for most of the night. Older revellers may find that the **Casino de Lanzarote** at Puerto del Carmen has some attractions. The gambling hall is open from 19:00 until 04:00. Gamblers have to be over 18 and an ID may be required to enter.

◀ *Left: Tasting wine at El Grifo Wine Museum near Masdache.*

FLOWER CARPETS

It is a common practice in Spain to make flower-petal patterns on the pavements for the **Corpus Christi** religious festival in late May or early June. In the Canary Islands it has become a fine art, with the designs being either geometric, floral or depicting scenes from the Bible. In Tenerife, coloured volcanic soil is used for the decoration, while in Gran Canaria they mainly stick to flowers. In Lanzarote, on the other hand, they use dyed salt for the patterns, reflecting their long tradition of salt production. Ironically, so little salt is produced on the island today that most of the material for the 'flower' carpets has to be imported!

Crafts

Tourists find a wide variety of crafts to take home as souvenirs. The production of craft articles is a major source of income for many of the rural villages of Lanzarote. Sadly, however, many of the items on sale in souvenir shops are cheap imitations from abroad, and this is a considerable threat to the survival of ancient craft skills on the island. Many of the handicrafts that are so admired by tourists were once essential to the daily agricultural way of life in past centuries.

Fine **woodwork** can be seen in the ornately carved balconies in the older towns and villages of Lanzarote, and on furniture, chests and carved figures. The making of *timples*, a traditional Canarian stringed instrument (*see* panel, page 31), is centred on Teguise. **Basketwork**, using wood, cane, straw, as well as palm and banana leaves, is a common craft throughout the island. Examples include fans, baskets and bags, while the finely woven straw hats from Yaiza and Tinajo make excellent souvenirs. The craft of pottery has its beginnings in Guanche times and it is still made in the traditional way – without using a wheel. The pots vary in size – from large urns that were used to store olive oil down to small vases and ashtrays. Look out for the tiny *Idolos de Tara* (Guanche-style figurines) and for the *pinterderas* (clay seals with an imprint or design) which were probably used as brooches. It is possible to visit the studios of some of Lanzarote's potteries and watch these skilled artisans at work. Probably the most attractive souvenirs (and the lightest to carry home) are the **textiles**. Exquisitely embroidered cloth is seen in the colourful national costumes that are worn at local festivals. Tablecloths, napkins and handkerchiefs are the most commonly displayed items. Look for the genuine articles at artisan shops. Other interesting craft souvenirs include rag dolls in national costume, lacework made by the island's nuns, and jewellery fashioned from olivine – a semiprecious volcanic mineral called 'peridot' when transformed into a polished stone. One of the best ways to find gifts is to visit

▶ *Opposite: One of the many wind sculptures and mobiles found in public places. They were designed by Cesár Manrique.*

one of the island's flea markets. The most popular is the Sunday morning market at Teguise, which attracts coach loads of tourists from all over the island. You will find, however, that goods made by foreigners living on Lanzarote far outnumber the local craft sold here. Other possibilities are the Pueblo Marinero centre at Costa Teguise on Friday evenings, and the Punta Limones centre at Playa Blanca on Wednesday mornings.

The Arts

Although the Guanches left numerous examples of wall paintings in caves, it took some time before any notable Canary Island **painters** emerged. Most of the 17th-, 18th- and 19th-century artists confined their work to religious themes and some of their paintings may be seen in churches on the island. One of the best-known artists was Néstor de la Torre (1887–1938), who specialized in murals and was responsible for a campaign to revive Canarian folk art and architecture.

The work of the versatile César Manrique – artist, sculptor, architect and environmentalist – can be seen throughout the Canary Islands and particularly in his native Lanzarote.

José Luján Pérez (1756–1815) is a renowned **sculptor** and his work can be seen in churches and cathedrals throughout the Canary Islands. Although the Guanches had no written language, **literature** has a long history in the Canary Islands. Indeed there is a well-known saying that 'the Canary Islands is a land of poets'. There have been many novelists and poets over the centuries, but most of them have had to move to the mainland to gain recognition for their work. Perhaps the best-known novelist was Benito Pérez Galdós (1843–1920) who hailed from Las Palmas, Gran Canaria.

CANARIAN WRESTLING

Lucha Canaria or Canarian wrestling has strict rules. There are two teams of 12 participants or *luchadores*. Two contestants at a time attempt to throw each other to the ground in the best of three competitions or *brega*. Only the soles of the feet must touch the ground. Canarian wrestling is not a violent sport, as punching and kicking are not allowed. Skill and balance are more important than weight and size. The team that wins the most *bregas* claims the overall match. The villages of Uga and Los Valles are particularly noted for their *luchadores*.

INTRODUCING LANZAROTE

There are some fine **museums and art galleries** in the Canary Islands, although Lanzarote is lacking in this respect. Undoubtedly the best art gallery to visit is the **International Museum of Contemporary Art** located in the 18th-century Castillo de San José overlooking the harbour in Arrecife. It has an excellent permanent collection and special exhibitions.

Music and Dance

Although the Canary Islands have not produced any well-known composers, classical music is taken seriously and concerts are always well supported. Traditional folk music and dancing are usually observed at fiestas. Dances include the lively *isa* and the more dignified *folia*. Occasionally the *tajaraste*, a dance believed to have its origins in Guanche times, may be performed. Traditional instruments, such as the *characas* (castanets) and the *timple* (which is like a five-stringed ukelele), accompany the dancing. Immigrants from Andalucía have introduced many dances, such as the *malagueña* and the *sevillaña*. The village of San Bartolomé is particularly famed for its folk music. Other popular music includes Latin American *salsa* rhythms.

Architecture

The Guanches, who were largely cave-dwellers, left
little legacy in the way of vernacular architecture.
The oldest buildings in Lanzarote date back to the
Spanish Conquest. Over several centuries, raids by
Barbary pirates and buccaneers from Spain's nautical
rivals reduced many of the older buildings to ruins.
Nevertheless, some of Lanzarote's ancient houses
are in a good state of preservation. The Gothic style
was on its way out at the time of the Conquest and
many of the early buildings, especially churches, were
constructed in the **Mudéjar** style, which had been
bequeathed to the Spaniards by the Moors. In
domestic design, the *Mudéjar* style encompasses
the need for water and protection from the sun. Most
houses are built around a central courtyard or *patio*,
often with a decorated well. In the larger houses, the
patio has shady trees and a colonnaded cloister. This
scheme was also common on the front of the house, with a
covered, columned walkway at ground level and a balcony
on the first floor. The balconies are made of wood and often
elaborately decorated. There are a few good examples of
this style in the older part of Teguise, the ancient capital
of Lanzarote, but due to the lack of timber on the island,
wooden balconies are not as common here as they are on
the western part of the archipelago. Artisans' houses from
this period are much simpler stone and whitewashed
buildings, with predominantly flat roofs. There is a simple
way to date the older houses in Lanzarote – up to the end
of the 17th century, windows were often placed at irregular
levels, but from the 17th century onwards, house façades
became symmetrical, with a door at the centre and equal-
sized and spaced windows. By the 16th century, the *Mudéjar*
style had been replaced by the intricate **Plateresque**, named
after the work of silversmiths and particularly evident in
carved doorways and ceilings. By the 19th century,
Portuguese Baroque had appeared – typified by iron rail-
ings on balconies. During the same period public buildings,

▲ *Above: An old traditional
door in need of attention.*
◄ *Opposite: Dancers in local
costume at a festival in
Teguise.*

The **carnaval** at Arrecife is a high-
light on the island's calendar.
Mostly held along the waterfront
promenade, the carnival lasts for
two weeks during February and
is a riot of music, dancing and
fireworks. It traditionally ends
with the Ceremony of the Dying
Sardine (*see* panel, page 28).
Another lively carnival is held at
Puerto del Carmen – all the settlements on the island join in the
fun in their own small way.

INTRODUCING LANZAROTE

▶ *Right: Traditional carved wooden balconies at Teguise.*
▶ ▶ *Opposite: A striking mural at the César Manrique Foundation.*

such as town halls and museums, were being constructed in the **Neoclassical** style. The early 20th century saw some interesting **Art Nouveau** buildings which were mainly the work of César Manrique. The second half of the century saw the growth of tourism in the Canary Islands and with it came some unattractive multi-storeyed apartment blocks. Fortunately, Manrique saw to it that Lanzarote largely resisted the spread of these eyesores.

FINDING A TOILET

Public toilets are non-existent in Lanzarote, but this is not a problem. Most people just nip into a restaurant or bar to use the facilities – it is normal practice and you do not have to be a customer. Toilet doors have the usual easily recognizable male and female signs. Do use the toilets when visiting any of the César Manrique institutions, as they are among the most luxurious and civilized that you will find anywhere in the world. In particular, do not miss the amazing male and female signs on the toilet doors at Manrique's Cactus Garden (*see* page 78).

The Influence of César Manrique

The remarkable César Manrique is undoubtedly Lanzarote's best-known son. He was born in Arrecife in 1919, but grew up in La Caleta de Famara on the northern coast of the island. He became a celebrated modern artist and worked abroad for many years, both in mainland Spain and in New York. When he returned to Lanzarote in the 1960s he was appalled at the development that had taken place on the island. He devoted the rest of his life to educating his fellow *Lanzaroteños* about the harmony of art, nature and landscape in order to prevent the unsightly development that was threatening his homeland. He had considerable influence over the island's *cabildos* (town councils) and managed to prevent high-rise buildings, so that no structure (except church towers) is built higher than a Canary palm.

He recommended that rural buildings have whitewashed walls, with green doors and window frames. Roadside hoardings were banned, as was the tipping of rubbish, while all electric cables were to be laid underground.

Manrique also made his own artistic contributions to the landscape. His sculptures and mobiles (such as that of **Monumento al Campesino**, situated near Mozaga) grace the scenery. He turned the caves at **Jameos del Agua** and the **Cueva de los Verdes** from foul-smelling rubbish tips into places of unique beauty, designed a remarkable restaurant on the **Islote de Hilario** volcano, converted the **Castillo de San José** at Arrecife into an art gallery and restaurant, and designed the extraordinary **Mirador del Río** with its fantastic views across to Isla Graciosa. Manrique was also responsible for the **Cactus Garden** at Guatiza. Typically, he wanted no financial recompense for his efforts and was quite happy just to see visitors as well as *Lanzaroteños* appreciate the unspoilt beauty of the island.

When Manrique moved to Haría in 1988 he presented his former home at Taro de Tahiche to the public. This remarkable villa was built within a series of huge volcanic bubbles. It is now the Manrique Foundation (*see* page 79) and is open to visitors. Manrique was tragically killed in a car accident in 1992 at the age of 72, but his achievements live on for all to appreciate.

MALPAÍS

Large parts of southern Lanzarote are covered with black lava flows and cinders known as *malpaís* or **badlands**. Despite the fact that many of these lava flows are nearly 300 years old they are almost completely devoid of vegetation. The reason for this is the climate. Lanzarote's arid weather, with little rain and no frost, has been unable to break down the rock into a soil. The only plants to be seen are lichens. Over a hundred species of these have been identified, with the white *sterocalum* being the most common. The spreads of black *picón* fare a little better with occasional clumps of euphorbia of the *tabaibales* family. Comparisons with the surface of the moon are not too far-fetched!

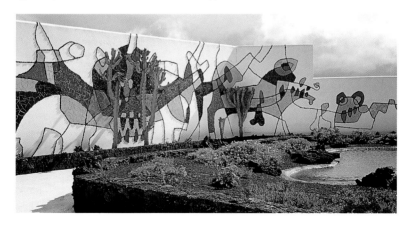

2
Arrecife

In Guanche times the coastal areas of Lanzarote were frequently raided by Berbers from North Africa and people were taken away to be used as slaves. The situation continued after the Spanish Conquest with the additional hazard of pirate raids from Spain's seafaring enemies. For this reason the capital of the island was located inland, at Teguise, where the inhabitants were safer. By the 19th century the island was a lot more peaceful due to its close links with the Americas. It was now important for a coastal town to be the main administrative settlement of the island. Thus, in 1824, Arrecife became the capital, although it is still known to locals as El Puerto. Arrecife (which means reef) gets its name from the numerous reefs of volcanic rock that lie offshore and protect the port.

Today, Arrecife is a typical Spanish working town and port with just over 55,000 inhabitants (2013 figures), many of whom travel to work at the main tourist resorts daily. Although it is not a particularly attractive place, Arrecife does not have the spread of high-rise apartment blocks which disfigure many Spanish cities. Instead, the suburbs consist mainly of single-storeyed houses in either a Canarian or Andalucían style. The town centre, however, is not particularly distinguished and few travel agents bother to arrange trips to Arrecife, although – for the more independent traveller with a hired car – the capital is well worth at least a half-day visit. It has a busy shopping centre, with shops selling goods at much cheaper prices than those in the resorts. It also has a

DON'T MISS

*** Castillo de San José: explore the castle that has been converted into a world-class modern art gallery by César Manrique.
** Castillo de San Gabriel: a sturdy defense fortress guarding the town.
* Charco de San Ginés: view a tidal inlet stretching into the heart of the town, lined with bars and shops.
* Iglesia de San Ginés: have a look at Arrecife's charming parish church.

◄ *Opposite: Small fishing boats in Arrecife's tidal Charco de San Ginés.*

ARRECIFE

couple of ancient castles, a few museums and art galleries, an interesting parish church, and a tidal lagoon that extends right into the middle of the town. The seafront, with its gardens and promenade, encourages an enjoyable stroll.

Parking, once a nightmare in Arrecife, is now much improved, with a string of parking lots along the seafront. Some are temporary, with unofficial parking attendants who are nevertheless very helpful and deserve a tip. The largest and safest parking area is underground parking beneath the Gran Hotel at the southern end of the seafront. The car parks fill up quickly, so get there as early as possible. The **tourist office**, housed in an interesting kiosk on the main promenade looking out to the Castillo, can provide a town plan but little else.

THE CENTRE
Castillo de San Gabriel ★★
A convenient first stop is the **Castillo de San Gabriel**, which is approached from Avenida Generalísimo Franco on the seafront by a pedestrian causeway. The castle, which was originally a wooden fortress, is actually built on a small

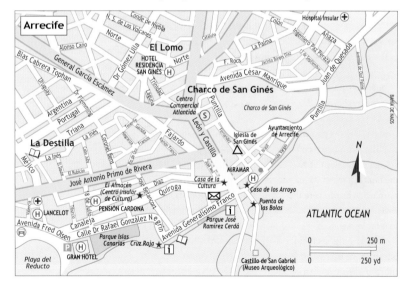

◄ *Left: Calle León y Castillo – the main pedestrian shopping street in Arrecife.*

rocky island called the Islote de los Ingleses. It was certainly not adequate to repel invaders, as it was eventually burnt down by Berber pirates. The castle was replaced in 1572 by a stone castle built by the Spaniard Sancho de Selín. It was reinforced in 1586 and again in 1590, but still found to be defective. Eventually it was completely rebuilt in 1592, during the reign of Felipe II, to the plans of the Italian fortress builder Leonardo Torriani (*see* panel, page 45).

Outside the castle, which is built with a pretty honey-coloured stone, are a couple of rusty old cannons. The interior once housed a modest archaeological museum. At the time of writing, the museum had been stripped out and all that can be seen are the impressive thickness of Torriani's walls and the low and narrow passageways. It is to be hoped that the museum will be reinstated in the near future.

From the castle's roof the skyline is dominated by the tall structure of the **Gran Hotel**. This is the only building on the island resembling a skyscraper. It was built while César

LEÓN Y CASTILLO

All the major towns of the Canary Islands seem to have a street or plaza named **León y Castillo**. Arrecife is no exception, since its main shopping street bears this name. Where did the name come from? It originates from two brothers who contributed a lot to the islands during their careers in the 19th and early 20th centuries. Fernando León y Castillo was a diplomat and politician who rose to the position of Foreign Minister of Spain and while in this job, he was able to obtain many dispensations for the islands. His brother, Juan, was an engineer and designed many projects in the Canaries. Their family home in Gran Canaria is now a museum.

Manrique was overseas and he was horrified by the sight on his return. He did not want further constructions of this kind on the rest of the island, so he persuaded the island's government to allow him to oversee future building developments on Lanzarote. The Gran Hotel was partially destroyed by fire in 1994 and remained as an eyesore for a number of years. It has recently been renovated and is now a luxury hotel with conference centre, popular restaurant and a galleria with jewellery and fashion shops. For superb views over the town and the surrounding volcanic landscape, take the lift to the 17th-floor snack bar for a restorative coffee. The hotel complex is surrounded by landscaped gardens and a children's play area, while boardwalks lead out to islands and the reef. The whole complex is a distinguished addition to the island's capital city.

Puente de las Bolas

Returning to the shore via the pedestrian causeway, you pass under the **Puente de las Bolas** (The Bridge of the Cannonballs), an old drawbridge named after the cannonballs

STREET SAFETY

Arrecife is probably the only town in Lanzarote where street crime might pose a problem. Most visitors to Lanzarote in general and Arrecife in particular will not have any difficulties at all, but it is wise to take a few sensible precautions: look out for pickpockets in crowded places such as markets and bus stations, avoid ill-lit areas late at night, leave all valuables in the hotel safe, remember to carry cash and credit cards in a body pouch, and do not leave any valuables on display in cars, as hired cars are easily recognizable.

on the top of its pillars. It has been adopted as the emblem of Lanzarote. Along the shoreline there are attractive gardens, known as the Parque José Ramírez Cerdá, with Canary palms, bougainvilleas and other colourful shrubs. The **Oficina de Turismo** is located here in a pleasant kiosk. The Norfolk Island palms to the side of the kiosk provide a roosting and nesting area for 50+ approachable cattle egrets.

Immediately opposite the bridge is Arrecife's main shopping street, Calle León y Castillo. Pedestrianized, it has most of the town's banks and a full range of shops, bars and restaurants, as well as the Centro Commercial Atlantida, which contains Lanzarote's largest department store. The island's *cabildo* (town council), with its attractive tiled frontage, is located on the right-hand side of Calle León y Castillo.

Iglesia de San Ginés ★

Turn right immediately after the *cabildo* along a narrow lane that leads to the shady square, the Plaza de Las Palmas. Here we find the parish church, the **Iglesia de San Ginés**. It was originally a 17th-century hermitage and became the parish church in 1798, dedicated to San Ginés, the patron saint of Arrecife.

Not Just a Fortress Builder

After continual raids by Berber pirates, Felipe II of Spain decided that the defences of the Canary Islands needed to be reorganized. He turned for assistance to the noted Genoese engineer and fortress builder **Leonardo Torriani**. Among the castles that he built or renovated on Lanzarote were the Castillo de San Gabriel in Arrecife and the Castillo de Santa Bárbara, built on the edge of a volcano overlooking Teguise. Torriani was not just an engineer, however, but also an observant historian. His book, *The Canary Islands and their Original Inhabitants* (1590), includes some wonderful descriptions and illustrations of the Guanches and their way of life. He also wrote a vivid account of the eruption of the Tegueso volcano on the island of La Palma.

◀ ◀ *Opposite: A cannon guards the entrance to Castillo de San Gabriel, which is now a museum.*
◀ *Left: The recently refurbished Gran Hotel, the only skyscraper on the island.*

ARRECIFE

The exterior is a pleasing combination of dark volcanic stone and whitewash, and the impressive square tower is capped with a belfry in the form of a gleaming white cupola. It is the dominant landmark of the town. The interior of the church is also full of interest. Simple black basalt columns lead to round arches of red volcanic material. The dark wooden ceiling is crafted in *Mudéjar* style, and the delicately painted pulpit with its spiral staircase is also made of wood. It is impossible to miss the symbolic modern painting, by Alberto Manrique; located behind the font, it depicts the fountain of life. It is also worth taking a quick look in the sacristy, where there is a large collection of religious statues. The church, and also the square outside it, are at the centre of the activities during Corpus Christi at Whitsun and the fiesta of San Ginés in August.

On returning to the Avenida Generalísimo Franco, we find a number of important buildings, including the *Ayuntamiento* (or town hall), the Miramar Hotel, and the police station. Also on the waterfront is the **Casa de los Arroyo**, which houses the Blas Cabrera Museum dedicated to the work of the well-known atomic scientist who was born in Arrecife. A small art gallery displays the work of local artist Pancho Lasso. The museum is open Monday to Friday (08:00–15:00); admission is free.

A side street leads to the town's *mercado*, a market selling fruit and vegetables, while on the opposite side of the road is a fascinating fish market.

Charco de San Ginés *

Further to the east is Arrecife's most attractive scenic feature, **Charco de San Ginés**, a tidal lagoon reaching into the heart of the town. It is said that San Ginés lived as a hermit on its shore. At low tide, wading birds prod among the mud and rocks, while at high tide colourful boats bob against the reflection of the buildings in the water, providing the opportunity to take beautiful photos. A promenade runs right around the *charco*, lined with palm trees, restaurants, bars and souvenir shops. The large modern building at the far end of the *charco* is a multi-screen cinema.

Manrique enthusiasts may want to seek out **El Almacén**, in Calle José Betancort, just off the western end of the Avenida Generalísimo Franco. This building was an old storehouse that César Manrique converted into an art gallery. It also has a bar, restaurant and bookshop.

THE EAST OF THE TOWN
Castillo de San José ★★★

Arrecife's only other sightseeing location requires some transport to reach. This is the **Castillo de San José** located in the east of the town. En route you will pass the port, and the first section is the **Puerto de Naos**, which is the harbour for fishing boats. Arrecife has the largest fishing fleet in the

▲ *Above: Iglesia de San Ginés, the parish church of Arrecife.*
◄ *Opposite: Puente de las Bolas, the Bridge of the Cannonballs, has become Lanzarote's emblem.*

▲ Above: *Charco de San Ginés, a tidal lagoon running into the heart of Arrecife.*
▶ Opposite: *The Castillo de San José was converted by César Manrique into a museum of modern art.*

Canary Islands and the seventh-largest in Spain. Fish is the basis of both the local canning and salting industries. You then reach the main commercial docks, the **Puerto de los Mármoles**, which is the second-largest port in the Canaries after Las Palmas and deals mainly with the container trade and cruise liners.

The **Castillo de San José** was built between 1776 and 1779, on the orders of King Carlos III, partly with the aim of defending the port against pirates. More importantly, it served to provide work and money for the *Lanzaroteños*, who had been suffering from starvation after the volcanic eruptions earlier in the century had destroyed their farmland. For this reason the castle became known as the *Fortaleza del Hambre* – the Hunger Fortress. For many years it acted as a powder and ammunition store, but by the 20th century it had become derelict. In 1968 César Manrique suggested that it should be renovated and converted into an art gallery. Work soon began and in 1976 it was opened as the **Museo Internacional de Arte Contemporáneo**. Manrique put together a collection of abstract art, including work by Tápies, Picasso, Miró and of course his own pictures, along with modern sculptures, many of which are outside the entrance.

SEEING IN THE NEW YEAR

It is the habit in Spain, including Lanzarote, to celebrate the New Year rather than Christmas. At the stroke of midnight on New Year's Eve it is the custom to drink *cava* (the Spanish version of champagne) and eat a grape for each strike of the clock. To consume 12 grapes and take a drink so quickly is not easy and it usually leads to great hilarity.

The castle has proved to be a unique setting for an art gallery, with the dark barrel-like ceilings of the 18th-century building contrasting with the bright and colourful paintings and sculptures. A spiral staircase leads down to Manrique's restaurant, the design of which he is said to have drawn directly onto the ground with chalk! The restaurant has dramatically modern black tables and chairs, and even black napkins, while a huge picture window looks out over the bustling container docks and cruise ships. As is usual with Manrique's schemes, the toilets are well worth a visit, with classical music accompanying your ablutions.

The Castillo de San José is open daily (10:00–20:00). The restaurant opens for lunch Tue–Sat and for dinner Fri–Sat; tel: 928 812321. There is an entrance fee for the art gallery. If you are just visiting the restaurant, take the path at the left-hand side of the castle.

THE VIRGEN DEL CARMEN FESTIVALS

The Virgen del Carmen is the patron saint of fishermen and seafarers. Each July the fishing villages around the coast of Lanzarote honour this saint with a spectacular festival. An image of the virgin is taken from the parish church and paraded around the streets, ending up at the beach or harbour. Here, she is briefly taken into the sea, either on the shoulders of the fishermen or on a boat, before being taken back to her sanctuary. The fiesta is accompanied by singing, dancing, fireworks and the cooking of giant paellas.

THE TOWN BEACHES

After a morning's sightseeing in Arrecife, what better and more relaxing way to spend the afternoon than to visit the town beaches – the **Playa del Reducto** and the **Playa del Cable**. They stretch from the town all the way to the airport and have been cleaned up to such an extent that they have earned Blue Flags.

ARRECIFE AT A GLANCE

BEST TIMES TO VISIT

Arrecife is pleasant place to visit at any time of the year, although a particularly interesting time to go to the capital is during the **Fiesta de San Ginés**, which takes place in the month of August and lasts for approximately a week. Also in August is the **Fiesta del Carmen**, when the celebrations include effigies of the saint being floated on the sea.

GETTING THERE

Regular **buses** run from the resorts to Arrecife, but they are not always reliable. Line 1 runs to Costa Teguise, line 22 to Puerto del Carmen and line 4 to the airport. **Taxis** are cheap, but hired **cars** are generally more convenient. The best place to park your car is along the waterfront or in the underground car park beneath the Gran Hotel. Try to arrive early, as the parking area becomes congested quickly. The tourist information office is conveniently situated on the sea front.

GETTING AROUND

The most attractive and interesting features of Arrecife are within walking distance from the main car park, although transport is necessary to visit Castillo de San José. Buses in the area run at half-hourly intervals and taxis are also available. The main taxi rank is situated opposite the Castillo de San Gabriel. There are other taxi ranks in Calle León y Castillo and Calle Pérez Galdós. For Radio Taxi, tel: 928 804608. The bus station is in Vía Medular.

WHERE TO STAY

Few tourists stay in Arrecife, as it is not necessary with the major resorts situated close by. Accommodation here is rather limited and generally caters for business people. Hotels on Lanzarote, as in the rest of the Islands, are given a star rating based on the various facilities that are offered and not the quality.

Luxury

Gran Hotel, Parque Islas Canarias, s/n, 35500 Arrecife de Lanzarote, tel: 928 800000, fax: 928 805906, www.aghotelspa.com Renovated luxury hotel overlooking the waterfront. Two restaurants, snack bar and spa.

Mid-range

Hotel Lancelot, Avenida Mancomunidad 9, tel: 928 805099, fax: 928039, www.hotellancelot.com Modern hotel overlooking the beach, with a pool and bar. **Hotel Villa Vik**, Urb. La Bufona, Playa del Cable, tel: 928 815256, fax: 928 817842, www.vikhotels.com Boutique hotel with contemporary decor a short walk from the city centre. **Hotel Diamar**, Avenida Fred Olsen 8, tel: 928 072481, www.hoteldiamar.es Mid-

sized simple hotel in the centre of the city. **Hotel Miramar**, Avenida Coll 2, tel: 928 812600, fax: 928 801533, www.hmiramar.com Modern hotel overlooking the seafront.

Budget

Inspect the room before making a reservation. **Pensión Cardona**, Calle 18 Julio 11, tel: 928 811008, fax: 928 817008. Central and close to the seafront. **Hotel Residencia San Ginés**, Calle del Molino 9, tel: 928 811 863. Another reasonably priced and cheerful option that is available to visitors.

WHERE TO EAT

There is a good range of traditional Canarian and international restaurants, but few genuine *tapas* bars remain in Arrecife.

Luxury

Castillo de San José, tel: 928 812321. Sophisticated food is served at this Manrique-designed restaurant in a converted castle overlooking the harbour. Best to make reservations well in advance. **Lilium**, Calle Jose Antonio 103, tel: 928 524978, www.restaurantlilium.com Excellent Spanish and European cuisine served with contemporary style.

Mid-range

Marisquería Mesoñ Los Troncos, Calle Agustin de la

Hoz 9, tel: 928 813637. Restaurant serving outstanding seafood, next to the Puerto de Naos.

Lancelot, Avenida Mancomunidad 9, tel: 928 805099. A hotel restaurant opposite El Reducto beach.

Taiwan, Calle Canalejas 52, tel: 928 805347. Moderately priced Chinese restaurant.

Casa Ginory, Calle Juan de Quesada 7, tel: 928 804046. A good seafood restaurant located close to the *charco*.

El Nuevo Maccheroni, Calle Jose Antonio Primo de Rivera 103, tel: 828 081325, www.elnuevomaccheroni.com Tasty Italian dishes and a good street-side terrace.

La Puntilla, Avenida de Cesar Manrique 52, tel: 928 816042, www.lapuntilla comidas.es Market fresh and seasonal products on the menu of the typical Canarian eatery.

Budget
Tapas Bars

One of the finest, and with the best ambience, is **San Francisco**, Calle León y Castillo 10, inside an atmospheric cellar. Another good option is **Tasca La Raspa** on the *charco*, with its traditional ambience. Other *tapas* bars include **Lemon Bar** and **Café Bar Minoca** alongside the *charco*. Visitors with a sweet tooth should try the **Pastelería Lolita**, just opposite the casino.

Shopping

Arrecife is probably the best place to shop on the island. Most of the shops are centred along Calle León y Castillo and its side streets. The prices here are a lot more reasonable than in the resorts. There is a Saturday morning market alongside El Charco de San Ginés. Manrique fans can buy goods with his designs and prints at the Tienda Fundación César Manrique, Calle José Betancourt 26. Local craftworks can be found in a number of artisan shops in the area. The best bookshop in Arrecife is Librería el Puente in Calle Insp. Luis Martín.

Useful Contacts

Oficina de Turismo, Parque Municipal, tel: 928 813174. The office is open Monday–Friday 09:30–17:00, Saturday 10:00–13:00. A number of firms offering adventure sports are based in Arrecife and their a ctivities include:

Hang-gliding, Clube de Parapente Los Cuervos, tel: 928 815426; and Delta Club Zonzamas, tel: 928 815203.

Water-skiing, Nautic Boat,

tel: 928 800007. This firm also offers **fishing** trips.

Paragliding, contact Fly Lanzarote, tel: 687 933122.

Windsurfing, Club de Windsurf Los Charcos, tel: 928 810894.

Diving, try the Club de Actividades Subacuaticas Pastinaca based at Playa Honda, south of Arrecife. The **main post office** is situated at La Marina 8. In the event of an **emergency** contact the main police station at Avenida del Coll 5. For multi-lingual help contact tel: 902 102112.

For **medical emergencies** call the Red Cross, tel: 928 812222. The **main hospital,** Doctor Jose Molina Oroso, is situated on the northwest side of the town on the San Bartolomé road, tel: 928 595000.

Entertainment

Arrecife can be quite lively in the evenings, with a number of clubs and bars along Calle José Antonio offering live music.

Teatro Atlantico offers a programme of live theatre, while **Multicines Atlántida** located on the shore of the *charco* is a multi-screen cinema.

ARRECIFE	J	F	M	A	M	J	J	A	S	O	N	D
AVERAGE TEMP. ºF	62.2	63.5	65.3	66.2	68.4	71.4	74.8	76.5	75.9	72.5	68.5	64.6
AVERAGE TEMP. ºC	17	17.5	18.5	19	20.2	21.9	23.8	24.7	24.4	22.5	20.3	18.1
HUMIDITY %	81	82	80	81	81	80	80	79	81	82	83	84
RAINFALL in	0.9	0.6	0.6	0.2	0.1	0	0	0	0.1	0.3	0.5	1
RAINFALL mm	24	14	15	6	2	0	0	0	2	7	12	27

3
The North
and the Islands

Scenically, the north of Lanzarote is the most fascinating part of the island. Like the south, it has areas where there has been recent volcanic activity, with large stretches of volcanic lava forming *malpaís*, but in general the eruptions happened earlier in historical time, so the lava and ash have had time to mature and form a reasonable soil. Farming in the north also benefits from a higher level of precipitation, as the area catches rain from the northerly trade winds.

There are also plenty of tourist attractions which include the famous tubes that formed in the lava flows from Mount Corona. The **Jameos del Agua**, adapted imaginatively by César Manrique, and the **Cueva de los Verdes**, where the Guanches used to hide from Berber pirates, both attract coach loads of visitors throughout the year. Manrique was also responsible for developing the **Mirador del Río**, which affords spectacular views of **Isla Graciosa** and the other islands to the north. There are two more *miradors* providing wonderful vistas at Guinate and Haría.

Although there are no large tourist resorts in the north of the island, there are a number of small fishing villages, such as **Arrieta** and **Orzola**, where delicious seafood can be found in restaurants with terraces looking out over the Atlantic. Orzola also provides a ferry service to Isla Graciosa. Despite the fact that most holiday-makers will be based in resorts in southern Lanzarote, they should make an effort to visit the north with its superb scenery and Manrique-inspired restaurants.

DON'T MISS

★★★ Jameos del Agua: Manrique's conversion of volcanic tubes into an concert hall, nightclub and pools.
★★★ Cueva de los Verdes: volcanic tubes under lava.
★★★ Mirador del Río: lookout point and restaurant designed by Manrique.
★★ Mirador de Guinate: viewpoint overlooking El Río and Isla de Graciosa.
★★ Mirador de Haría: a mountain pass with great views.
★★ Parque Tropical: over 1300 species of birds and animals.

◀ *Opposite: Jameos del Agua, Manrique's conversion of volcanic tubes and bubbles.*

THE NORTH AND THE ISLANDS

ARRIETA AND SURROUNDS

The road north from Arrecife meets the coast at Arrieta, a small, unpretentious fishing village. The roundabout at the entrance to the village is graced by a striking red wind sculpture by César Manrique, and the area in the vicinity is now seeing a modest amount of development. Arrieta has a small harbour and an equally small sandy beach called the Playa de la Garita. Here there are several fish restaurants that tempt the visitor, but prices are not cheap.

Just north of Arrieta is a small, and quite unspoilt, fishing settlement called **Punta de Mujeres**. This village marks the start of the **Malpaís de la Corona**, an area of badlands that stretches north for the next 10km (6.2 miles) to Orzola. This volcanic lava flowed out of **Mount Corona**, which can be seen to the west, rising to some 609m (2000ft). Although the eruption took place between 5000 and 6000 years ago, there is remarkably little vegetation on the surface of the lava, apart from white lichens and a few clumps of spurges. The *malpaís* is famous for being the location of one of the longest **lava tubes** in the world. Known as the Atlantic Tube System, the tube runs southeast from the volcano for 7.5km (4.7 miles), and the last 1km (0.6 mile) is under the sea

Northern Lanzarote

Roque del Infierno o del Oeste
Montaña Clara 256 m
Isla de Montaña Clara
Punta Gorda
Baja de la Majapalomas
Montaña Bermeja 157 m
Playa Lambra
Punta del Hueso
Parque Natural de los Islotes del Norte de Lanzarote y Riscos de Famara
Punta de Petro Barba o de la Sonda
Isla Graciosa
Agujas Chicas ▲257 m
Pedro Barba
Punta de la Baja
Agujas Grandes 266 m
Caleta de Pedro Barba
Montaña del Mojón 188 m
Baja del Ratón
Punta Fariones
Caleta del Sebo
El Río
Playa de la Canteria
El Embarcadero
Montaña Amarilla 172 m
Bahía del Salado
Salinas del Río
Batería
Orzola
Charca de la Laja
Mirador 179 m
Caletón Blanco
Playa del Risco del Río
Las Pardelas
Bajo de los Sables
El Embarcadero
Casas la Breña
Yé
La Caleta
Mirador de Guinate
Parque Tropical
Las Rositas
Monte Corona
Haría
Punta del Roque
Guinate 609 m
Los Helechos
La Quemada ▲ 581 m
562 m
Los Lomillos
Máguez
La Atalaya
Punta de Piquinto
Cueva de los Verdes★
Jameos★ del Agua
Punta Usaje
Punta de Gaya
Los Castillejos
Punta de Mujeres
Los Caletones
Punta Ganada
Museo Internacional de Miniaturas
Punta del Burro
Los Mariscales
Las Bajas
Caleta del Campo
Los Morros
Playa de Famara
Mirador de Haría
Arrieta
Playa de la Garita
Peñas del Chache 670 m
Tabayesco
Morro el Lajero
Risco del Lajero
Mirador del Valle
Presa de Mala
Punta de la Pared
Ermita de las Nieves ★
Teguise
Mala
Playa del Seifio
Parque Eólico Wind Farm
Risco Negro
GUATIZA
TEGUISE
MALPAÍS DE LA CORONA
RISCO DE FAMARA
LZ-10
LZ-1
LZ-10
N
0   4 km
0   2 miles

bed. Occasionally the tube widens out and forms 'bubbles' or caves. These include two of the most popular tourist attractions on the island.

▲ *Above: Lobster sculpture at the entrance to the Jameos del Agua.*

The Jameos del Agua ★★★

This complex of caves and partially collapsed tubes has been adapted by César Manrique to form the most remarkable showpiece on Lanzarote. (A *jaméo* is the name for a cavity produced when the roof of a volcanic tube collapses.) Just outside the complex is a huge sculpture of a lobster, similar to the illustration in Torriani's 16th-century book. A few steps at the entrance lead down into a bar that doubles as a nightclub on certain evenings of the week. The route leads into a large cavern containing a salt-water lake, thought to be the water that has filtered through the rocks. The lake's only inhabitants are small, blind, albino crabs (*Munidopsis polymorpha*) that average 3mm (0.12in) in length. How they got into the cave is unclear as their normal habitat is in deep-sea water. A notice requests that you do not throw coins in the water as the copper can adversely affect the crabs. Emerging from the cavern, you enter a contrasting world of lush plants,

CLIMATE

There is the possibility of light rain and even mist on the hills during the winter months when it can be quite cool, but for the rest of the year it should be warm and dry. The north is windier than the south of the island, particularly during the hotter summer months.

THE NORTH AND THE ISLANDS

▶ *Right: Lush vegetation surrounds this pool at Jameos del Agua, one of Lanzarote's most popular attractions.*

including palms and bougainvilleas, set around a deep blue pool with whitewashed surrounds. It is said that the King of Spain is the only person allowed to swim in the pool. At the far end of the pool is another cavern containing an auditorium with 550 seats, which is frequently used for concerts and shows. The whole place is awe-inspiring and many visitors feel the need to sit for a while and contemplate, while they soak up the atmosphere of this unusual location.

From the poolside, zigzag steps lead up to a terrace with a café and more Manrique toilets. The terrace leads to a superb museum, the **Casa de la Vulcanes**, with hi-tech, hands-on features that will thrill and inform everyone from children to pensioners. Before leaving this extraordinary place, stroll down a boardwalk over the *malpaís* to the sea, observing how the plants are struggling to survive among the hostile lava. This area is also a good spot for a picnic.

The Jameos del Agua are open daily Sun–Fri 10:00–18:30, Sat 10:00–22:00; tel: 928 848020. The bars are open during the day and also in the evening along with the restaurant on Tuesday, Friday and Saturday, when there is a nightclub and occasional folklore performances.

UNWELCOME VISITORS

Occasionally bodies are washed up on the east coast of Lanzarote and neighbouring Fuerteventura. These are Africans who have been attempting, illegally, to gain entry into EU countries in an effort to find a better life. The usual route is across the Straits of Gibraltar into mainland Spain, but the Spanish police are making this more difficult. Now these illegal immigrants, known as *clandestinos*, are risking the longer sea route to the eastern Canary Islands. Their boats are often inadequate and sadly many of the would-be immigrants drown.

Cueva de los Verdes ★★★

A short distance away is the rival attraction, **Cueva de los Verdes**. The word *verde* means green in Spanish, but there is nothing green about the cave – it was once owned by people by the name of Verde. Tour guides often, in fact, call it Green's cave. The whole place is a complex of caves at various levels, opening out into occasional caverns, one of which is large enough to host concerts – although one is mystified as to how the musicians get some of their bulkier instruments through the narrow tunnels. These caves are unlike those in limestone areas, which are often dripping with water and festooned with stalactites and stalagmites. Their attraction lies in the colour of the volcanic rocks, accentuated by clever lighting and atmospheric music. The caves have been known about for many centuries and they were used by local people to hide from invaders, such as pirates and slave traders. The Cueva de los Verdes is open daily (Oct–Jun 10:00–18:00, Jul–Sep 10:00–19:00). Guided tours run half-hourly and last for about an hour. The walk is quite demanding in places.

> **LAVA TUBES**
>
> When volcanic lava is of the thick and viscous kind, such as that which flowed out of Mount Corona and formed the *malpaís* of northeastern Lanzarote, **volcanic tubes** can be quite common. They are formed when the surface lava cools, but at lower levels the lava continues to flow and eventually leaves a cave-like tube or pipe behind. These tubes can frequently be followed for many kilometres and often widen out into large caverns.

◀ *Left: The Cueva de los Verdes is a complex of caves and caverns located in a lava flow.*

THE NORTH AND THE ISLANDS

ORZOLA

The coast road continues northwards through the *malpaís*. If cars are parked by the roadside, this usually indicates that there is a secluded beach nearby. There is a series of small, white sand beaches, known collectibely as **Caleton Blanco**. The sand in these coves is light in colour and makes a striking contrast with the dark volcanic rocks. The road eventually arrives at **Orzola**, the most northerly village in Lanzarote. It is a sleepy fishing settlement and noted for its seafood restaurants, many of which have terraces overlooking the harbour. Reefs of volcanic rock protect the harbour and this is not a safe area to swim or dive in rough weather. There is a good sandy beach, however, just to the north called Playa de la Cantería. Ferries run several times a day from Orzola to Isla Graciosa. A variety of other boats bob around in Orzola's harbour, including sport-fishing craft and a glass-bottomed boat for underwater viewing. Visitors arriving by car should note that parking can be difficult in the village, particularly at weekends when hordes of locals swarm in to sample the seafood restaurants. There is free parking at the port where you can leave the car if you are taking the ferry across to Isla Graciosa.

YÉ AND SURROUNDS

A spectacular mountain road now leads across to the town of Yé. This strange place name appears to have meant 'the end of the earth' in the Guanche language. It was once an important centre for extracting purple dye from lichen, but today its main claim to fame is the remarkable skill of its wrestlers.

Mirador del Río ★★★

We now reach another of Lanzarote's locations that cannot be missed, the **Mirador del Río**. This, again, is the work of César Manrique. In 1974, with his typical flair, he converted an old gun emplacement some 497m (1630ft) above sea level into a restaurant and viewing platform. From the car park the place initially looks uninspiring, with a drab convex curve of volcanic block merging into the hillside, but –

inside – a narrow passage leads to a restaurant, dominated by two of Manrique's ceiling sculptures. Picture windows lead to a semi-circular viewing platform providing one of the best vistas in the Canary Islands. Down beneath the steep cliffs is the abandoned saltworks of the **Salinas del Río**, with its subtle pink water. Then, further out, is **El Río**, which is not a river at all, but the strait that separates Isla Graciosa from the mainland. The island itself looks barren, with just one small settlement, **Caleta del Sebo**, a small marina, some sand dunes and a few extinct volcanoes. Away in the distance other islands can be seen, such as **Montaña Clara** and **Alegranza**, which are inhabited only by sea birds. It is necessary to pay for entrance to the *mirador*, which is open daily (July–Sep 10:00–18:45, 10:00–17:45 rest of year).

GUINATE
Mirador de Guinate ★★

If you don't like the idea of paying the entrance fee to the Mirador del Río, then all is not lost – head southwards to the village of **Guinate**. Turn right and proceed towards the sea. Just past the Parque Tropical is the **Mirador de Guinate**, which has no entrance fee and arguably provides even better views than does the Mirador del Río. Look out for the hang-

▲ *Above: Another striking Manrique sculpture marks the entrance to the Mirador del Río.*

TREASURE ISLAND

Isla Graciosa, to the north of Lanzarote, is dry and barren. It is many people's idea of the archetypal desert island. So perhaps it is inevitable that there are stories of buried treasure on Isla Graciosa. One such tale concerns an English ship that was chased to the island by pirates. The crew managed to bury their treasure before they were killed. However, the ship's cabin boy survived and fled back to England. He never revealed the location of the treasure until he was very old, but by then he was too senile to remember the exact spot.

THE NORTH AND THE ISLANDS

▶ *Right: A peacock struts his stuff at the Parque Tropical at Guinate.*

gliders and paragliders, who enjoy the updraughts caused by the winds beating against the towering cliffs of the **Risco de Famara**.

Parque Tropical ★★

The other reason for stopping at Guinate is to visit the **Parque Tropical**. Covering some 45,000m², the park claims to have over 1300 rare and exotic birds and animals. Many birds breed in the large aviaries, while others, such as peacocks, roam free. There is a huge walk-through aviary and in the lush vegetation you can see weaver birds busily building their hanging nests. There are numerous streams, waterfalls and ponds full of enormous koi carp. The strange and eclectic range of animals on offer includes heat loving crocodiles and cold resistant penguins. The park also has some monkeys and lemurs, having been brought here after being rescued from illegal owners. A firm favourite with children is the parrot show, which is held six times a day. These colourful birds (actually sulphur-crested cockatoos and blue macaws) perform tricks such as pulling toy carts, driving model pick-up trucks and riding toy bicycles. Parque Tropical is open daily (10:00–17:00); there is an admission fee; tel: 928 835500, www.guinatetropicalpark.com

HARÍA

The road continues southwards to **Haría**, which is the main town of northern Lanzarote and certainly one of the most attractive villages on the island. Part of its allure is the unexpected abundance of trees, and tour guides often refer to the area as the 'valley of a thousand palms'. A local legend suggests that a palm tree was planted for every girl born here and two for each boy, but the truth may be more prosaic – the palms are most probably the remains of a 16th-century plantation. Haría and the surrounding valley certainly look green and fertile, particularly after the winter rains which produce a wealth of wild flowers. The town itself has around 3000 inhabitants and is full of interest, with its numerous craft shops where artisans can be seen at work. It does not come as a surprise to learn that César Manrique chose to retire in Haría. The beating heart of Haría is the **Plaza León y Castillo**, a pretty cobbled square shaded by mature trees and flanked by whitewashed cottages. There's a lively market here on Saturday mornings selling fruit, vegetables and handicrafts. The small parish church of **Nuestra Señora de la Encarnación** was rebuilt in the 1950s and houses a small museum of sacred art (Museo de Arte Sacro).

Mirador de Haría ★★

For the best view of the town of Haría, travel southwards and climb the pass that leads to the **Mirador de Haría**. There are two bar-restaurants that are popular stops for coaches, and both give spectacular vistas. The great number of palm trees in and around Haría can easily be picked out. Away to the east is the broad valley of Temisa, with a number of abandoned terraces on its flanks, leading down to Tabayesco and Arrieta on the coast. To the south there is the obtrusive hulk of **Peñas del**

Chache, which at a height of 670m (2198ft) is Lanzarote's highest mountain.

A DAY TRIP TO ISLA GRACIOSA

For anyone looking for a spot of peace and quiet, a day trip to Isla Graciosa is an interesting possibility. The island was, in fact, Jean de Béthencourt's first landfall in the Canary Islands. He was the Norman who first conquered Lanzarote. Isla Graciosa can be reached by ferry from Orzola and there are several daily crossings in both directions by modern launch. The crossing takes 15–30 minutes. There are no roads on Isla Graciosa and therefore no cars, but the main settlement, Caleta del Sebo, has a couple of simple *pensiónes* (boarding/guest houses) and some basic restaurants. Lunch at one of these restaurants can be booked in advance when purchasing the ferry ticket. A track links Caleta del Sebo with Pedro Barba, the only other settlement

▼ *Below: Part of the attractive town of Haría, with some of its many palm trees.*

◄ *Left: The view from the Mirador del Río shows Isla Graciosa, with its complex of volcanoes.*

on the island which is only populated during the summer months. There are only around 600 permanent residents on the island and most of them are involved in fishing. As Isla Graciosa covers a mere 25km² (9.7 square miles), it is quite possible to walk around the island in a day, using the footpath that follows the shore. Mountain bikes can also be hired at the port. The scenery consists largely of deserted sandy beaches, sand dunes, barren plains and the cones of four extinct volcanoes: Agujas Chicas at 257m (843ft), Agujas Grandes at 266m (872ft), Montaña del Mojón at 188m (606ft) and Montaña Bermeja at 157m (515ft). Graciosa and the other islands were designated a national marine reserve in 1995. Isla Graciosa is the perfect place to experience a tranquil day out! For those who want to stay longer and experience a true getaway holiday, book a room at a pensión in Caleta del Sebo, or alternatively there are several houses and apartments for rent.

TO TIP OR NOT TO TIP?

It is always important to know whether or not tipping is expected. In the Canary Islands a tip (*una propina*) is always appreciated, but don't pay up unless the service is good. In restaurants, check the bill to see if the service charge is included. If not, it is usual to add between 5 and 10 per cent. In cafés and bars, some loose change is normally sufficient. Porters in airports and hotels generally expect a small tip. On excursions, coach drivers and guides are normally rewarded if they have provided a good service.

BEST TIMES TO VISIT

The north is generally cloudier than the south of Lanzarote, so choose a clear day to visit the area. It can also be very breezy as it receives the full force of the trade winds. The northern beaches may be remote and with few people but the blown sand can make things uncomfortable, while the ocean currents can be dangerous, particularly beneath the cliffs of Famara.

GETTING THERE

Buses run from Arrecife to Orzola and Haría four times a day (line 9) and link with the ferry to Isla Graciosa, but service can be unreliable. **Coach** tours visit the major sites, but rarely allow sufficient time for leisurely sightseeing. A hired **car** is most convenient.

GETTING AROUND

The few major roads in the north are in good condition and signposting is clear, so those with hired cars should have few problems. Some minor roads and rough tracks, however, are in poor conditions and should be avoided. Remember that petrol stations can be few and far between.

WHERE TO STAY

Good accommodation is virtually non-existent in the north of Lanzarote, since both Arrecife and the main southern holiday centres are within reach. There are a few *pensiónes* on **Isla Graciosa** and a few apartments and bungalows elsewhere.

Budget

Pensión Enriqueta, Calle de la Mar Barlovento 6, Caleta del Sebo, tel: 928 842051. Next to the harbour, restaurant.
Pensión Girasol, Harbour, Caleta del Sebo, tel: 928 842 118. Restaurant and some rooms with a sea view.
Apartamentos La Graciosa, tel: 928 842103, www.apartmentosgraciosa.com Has several village houses in Caleta del Sebo.
Casitas del Mar, www.casitas-del-mar.com Small bungalows can be hired at this modest complex north of Arrieta.

Rural Accommodation

Two are highly recommended:
Casa La Ermita, 35520 Mágnez, Haría, tel: 928 842 535, fax: 928 842535. Simple apartments with pool; bikes for hire.
Finca La Corona, Calle Las Rositas, Yé, Haría, tel/fax: 928 528019. Apartments with pool. For permission to **camp** on Isla Graciosa contact the *ayuntamiento* in Caleta del Sebo, tel/fax: 928 842000.

WHERE TO EAT

There is a wide choice of places to eat in the area, particularly in Arrieta and Orzola. There are also a number of restaurants, mainly inland, where traditional Canarian food can be found.

Arrieta

This fishing village has a number of excellent restaurants near the harbour.

Mid-range

Casa Miguel, Calle de Noria, tel: 928 848646. This well-established quayside restaurant is full of atmosphere; selection of traditional local seafood.
El Charcón, Calle de Noria, tel: 928 848110, www.elcharconlanzarote.com Quayside restaurant serving traditional dishes.
Jameos del Agua, tel: 928 848020. Many visitors to Jameos del Agua will find it convenient to eat here. There is an excellent snack bar open daily and a good restaurant open on Tue, Fri and Sat evenings to coincide with the folklore shows. Open from 19:00–02:00, with the show taking place at 23:00.
El Lago, Calle Los Morros 27, tel: 928 848176. Fish restaurant with seawater fish pond inside.
Restaurant el Marinero, La Garita 60, tel: 928 848382. Excellent fresh fish at one of the smarter restaurants along the seafront.

Orzola

Small fishing village and ferry port with plenty of seafood restaurants.

Mid-range

Perla del Atlantico, Avenida de Caleton, tel: 928 842589. Harbourside restaurant serves delicious fresh fish.
Punta Fariones, Calle de la

Quemadita, tel: 928 842558. Overlooks ferry quay, serves high-quality fish dishes.
Bahía de Orzola, Calle la Quemadita 6, tel: 928 842575. Good choice for fresh seafood.

Budget
Casa Arraez, Avenida de Caleton, Orzola, tel: 928 842523. Don't be put off by the rustic nature of this establish-ment. The fish is fresh and the price is a bargain. There are one or two restaurants away from the harbour. When the main restaurants are full, **El Norte** is worth a try.

Mirador del Río
Luxury
Mirador del Río, tel: 928 546548. Striking Manrique-designed eatery overlooking Isla Graciosa.

Haría
There are two restaurants on the Mirador del Valle pass, both with superb views.
Mid-range
Los Helechos, tel: 928 835 817. Canteen-style eatery, popular with coach parties.
Mirador del Valle, tel: 928 528036. Simple country café with a view, halfway down the pass.
The town of Haría also has a number of restaurants, many of which serve traditional Canarian dishes.

El Cortijo, Teguise road on the southern edge of the village, tel: 928 835686. Old farm-house serves traditional food

and is popular with the locals.
Los Cascajos, Calle Ferrer 9, Haría, tel: 928 835471, www. restauranteloscascajos.com Rural restaurant to the north of the town; produces its own wines.
Casa 'l Cura, Calle Nueva 1, Haría, tel: 928 835556. The local stews are recommended in this rural house.
Restaurant Meson la Frontera, Calle Casas de Atras 4, tel: 928 835310. Good barbecued meats and Canarian dishes.
La Puerta Verde, Calle Fajardo, Haría, tel: 928 835373. Probably the town's best tapas bar.

TOURS AND EXCURSIONS
Artesanía de Haría, Calle Barranco 4, Haría. Good range includes embroidery, basket-ware, silverware, pottery and artefacts made from volcanic rocks and minerals.
Taller de Artesanía, near the southern entrance of Haría. Woodcarvers, potters, silver-smiths and other craftsmen can be seen at work.

SHOPPING
Taller de Artesanía de Haría, Calle Barranco de Tenesía, has many traditional crafts under one roof and you can watch the artisans and artists at work.

USEFUL CONTACTS
Costanoroeste surfing and kiteboarding school based at Caleta de Famara, tel/fax: 928 528597,

www.costanoroeste.com
Graciosa Sail offers a full day aboard a luxury catamaran with lunch and opportunity to swim and snorkel, tel: 928 842585.
Ferry to Isla Graciosa. Contact **Lineas Martimas Romero**, tel: 928 842055, fax: 982 842069. For information contact the **ferry company** at Avenida Virgen del Mar 119A, Isla de La Graciosa, www.lineas romero.com
The timetable is as follows:
Summer (July-mid Oct)
Orzola to La Graciosa 08:30, 10:00, 11:00, 12:00. 13:30, 16:00, 17:00, 18:00, 20:00
La Graciosa to Orzola: 08:00, 08:40, 10:00, 11:00, 12:30, 15:00, 16:00, 17:00, 19:00.
Winter
Orzola to La Graciosa 08:30, 10:00, 11:00, 12:00. 13:30, 16:00, 17:00, 18:00, 19:00
La Graciosa to Orzola: 08:00, 08:40, 10:00, 11:00, 12:30, 15:00, 16:00, 17:00, 18:00.
Biosfera Express, tel: 928 842585, (www.bios feraexpress.com) also operates a similar service. The ferry generally takes about 15–30 minutes for the crossing. In very strong winds it may be cancelled. No boats run to the tiny uninhabited islands of Roque del Este, Roque del Oeste, Isla de Montaña Clara and Isla de Alegranza. These islands are offical nature reserves and landing on them is forbidden.

4
Central Lanzarote

Although Central Lanzarote cannot boast the spectacular scenery found in the north and south of the island, the area is full of interest. Right in the centre is **Teguise**, the old capital of Lanzarote, which is full of ancient churches and noble homes. It has a dignified atmosphere, which is disturbed only on Sundays by a market that attracts visitors from all over island.

The coastline of the central area of the island is largely undeveloped, with the notable exception of **Costa Teguise**, a purpose-built resort with Lanzarote's oldest golf course and aquapark. Fans of **César Manrique** have much to see, with the **Monumento al Campesino**, the **Fundación** in his former home, and the **Cactus Garden** on the outskirts of Guatiza.

Central Lanzarote is also one of the more fertile parts of the island, supporting numerous well-cared-for agricultural villages such as **Mozaga**, famous for its grapes; **Guatiza**, which is the centre of the cochineal industry; and **Tinajo**, specializing in onion and tomato cultivation. Many of these villages have unique and interesting little churches and hermitages. Museums include the award-winning **Museo Agrícola El Patio**, near Tiagua, and the imaginative Manrique-inspired **Casa Museo del Campesino**, near Mozaga. A most surprising feature on the north coast is the world-famous sports complex of **La Santa**, which offers so many sporting activities – such as tennis, sailing, sailboarding and athletics – that it is mentioned in the *Guinness Book of Records*. Many national teams come here to train.

DON'T MISS

*** **Teguise's Sunday market:** at the ancient capital.
*** **Fundación César Manrique:** see a remarkable house built into a series of volcanic bubbles.
*** **Jardín de Cactus:** Manrique's garden of cacti at Guatiza with over 1400 species.
*** **Museo Agrícola El Patio:** prize-winning museum of country life.
** **Castillo de Santa Bárbara:** visit the castle perched on the lip of a volcanic crater. Now a museum.

◀ *Opposite: The Jardín de Cactus, Manrique's imaginative use of an old quarry.*

CENTRAL LANZAROTE

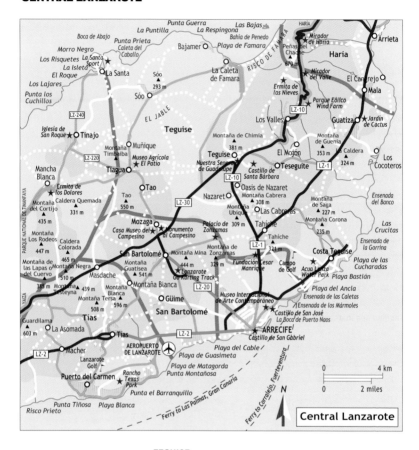

Central Lanzarote

TEGUISE

Teguise was the ancient capital of Lanzarote from the days of Maciot de Béthencourt up until 1852, when the administration was transferred to Arrecife. Teguise was, in fact, named after Béthencourt's wife, who was the daughter of Guardafía, the last of the Guanche leaders. Founded in 1418, Teguise was often referred to as the *Villa Real* (the royal city), a term still used by many *Lanzaroteños*, who dismiss Arrecife as *El Puerto* (the port). The Béthencourt dynasty was followed by the Los Herreras family and then, between the 16th and

18th centuries, Teguise developed as a fine colonial town with some impressive churches, convents and domestic architecture. However, during these times there was always the danger of being raided by Berber pirates. The small alleyway at the side of the parish church is known as the *Callejon de la Sangre* (the alley of blood) after large numbers of women and children were slaughtered here in a raid in 1586. After Arrecife became the capital of Lanzarote, the glory of Teguise faded somewhat, but during the 1980s a restoration programme was undertaken, with the encouragement of César Manrique.

Plaza de San Miguel

Nowadays, the charm of Teguise lies in its quiet and dignified streets. At the centre of things is the **Plaza de San Miguel** (officially called the Plaza de la Constitución), with its fountain and Norfolk Island pines guarded by two imposing stone lions. Dominating the square is the parish church, the **Iglesia de San Miguel**, also known as the Iglesia de Nuestra Señora de Guadalupe. It has a bell tower of brown volcanic rock capped with a white octagonal belfry. The rest of the exterior is white with

▼ *Below: Teguise's distinctive parish church, Iglesia de San Miguel, overlooks the Plaza de la Constitución.*

CENTRAL LANZAROTE

▶ *Opposite: The ancient capital of Teguise seen from the rim of the volcano Guanapay.*

CLIMATE

Located between the windier, wetter north and the sunnier, arid south, central Lanzarote can be said to have the average climate of the island. In January the mean temperatures are 17°C (63°F) with 50mm (2in) of rain, but by July, temperatures have risen to 25°C (77°F) and rainfall is rare.

dark stone corners. Do admire the stone doorway on the south side. The church was damaged by pirates on numerous occasions and suffered a further blow in the early 20th century when it was ravaged by fire, leading to extensive renovation. The interior is light with much white plasterwork. Note the pillars of dark volcanic stone, the rounded arches and the painted ceiling. Remember that the church, together with most of the other monuments in Teguise, closes in the afternoons.

On the south side of Plaza de San Miguel, there is a small building known as **La Cilla**. It was once a tithe barn, where the payments were collected from the local farmers and paid to the Bishop of Gran Canaria. After falling into disrepair, it was renovated in the mid 1980s.

On the west side of the plaza is the **Palacio Spínola**. More a town house than a palace, it was built in the mid-18th century and made from blocks of lava and timber supports. After being occupied by various noble families, it came into the hands of the Río Tinto company, who agreed to restore it. The *palacio* was then bought by the town council in 1984 and converted into a museum. In 1989 it was made the official residence of the Governor of the Canary Islands when he or she is in Lanzarote. Today it has been transformed into the Timple Museum, with a large selection of these typical Canarian musical instruments. It also houses occasional art and cultural exhibitions. The

Teguise

0   200 m

0   200 yd

Calle Norte
Ermita de La Vera Cruz
Calle Timanfaya
Plaza de La Reina Ico
Archivo Histórico
Casa Cuartel
Calle Puerto y Villa de Garachico
Correo
Parque la Mareta
Plaza Clavijo y Fajardo
Plaza Maciot de Béthencourt
18 de Julio
La Cruz
Guardería
Universidad
Iglesia de Nuestra Señora de Guadalupe (Iglesia de San Miguel)
Nueva
Casa Palacio Torres Spínola
Plaza de la Constitución
Notas
Plaza San Miguel
Casa del Marqués
Teatrillo
La Cilla
Casa Parroquial Herrera-Rojas
Palacio Reyes Catolicos
Calle Marqués de Herrera
Plaza de San Francisco
Calle José Betancort
Plaza Camilo José Cela
Plaza Doctor Alfonso Spínola
Convento de San Francisco
Calle Gran Canaria
Convento de Santo Domingo
Plaza General Franco
Ayuntamiento
Avenida Gran Aldea
HARIA: CASTILLO DE SANTA BARBARA
ARRECIFE
N

Palacio Spinola is open Monday-Saturday 09:00-16:30 and Sunday 09:30-15:30, www.casadeltimple.org

Convents

Teguise has two important convents, one being the **Convento de San Francisco**, which was built by Franciscan missionaries in the late 16th century, although the convent's church is all that remains today. The exterior has some fine stonework including an unusual spiral pattern over the main door. The interior has two naves, one larger than the other, and the decoration is mainly *Mudéjar* in style. The most attractive features are the three altarpieces, a carved wooden pulpit, and a font made of volcanic stone. The Convent of San Francisco is now the Sacred Art Museum and is open from Monday to Friday 09:00 and 15:00 (except Tuesdays), and on Saturdays and Sundays between 09:30 and 14:00. The **Convent of Santo Domingo** can be found in the southwest of Teguise and is believed to have been founded in 1726. Renovations began in the 1980s, but were abruptly halted when over 100 partly mummified skeletons (possibly of Guanche origin) were found in the crypt.

WOODEN BALCONIES

There is a long tradition of woodcarving in the Canary Islands, both in craftwork and in the Plateresque style of carving found in church interiors dating from the 16th and 17th centuries. The wetter, western Canary Islands have plenty of Canary pine available, and inevitably the detailed carving style spread into domestic architecture. The pine is easily carved, but also very durable and best seen in the intricate balconies of fine mansions. Lanzarote, unfortunately, with its arid climate, does not have many Canary pine trees, so all the timber had to be imported. Ornate balconies, therefore, were mainly confined to the wealthy townhouses and *palacios* of Teguise, where they were status symbols.

▲ Above: Traditional dancing in Teguise attracts tourists from all over the island.

Domestic Buildings

Teguise has a number of domestic buildings of note. **Casa Torres** dates from the 18th century. **Palacio Herrera-Rojas** once housed the island's archives, but they were destroyed by Berber pirates, and it now has an art gallery. **Casa Parroquial** was a barracks in the 17th century, while **Casa Cuartel** was once a prison. The architecture of the domestic buildings is typified by corners of black or red volcanic stone, with whitewashed walls and varnished wooden doors and windows. The occasional balcony and traditional chimney can also be seen. Another interesting part of Teguise can be found at the back of the parish church. This is the **Parque la Mareta**, which was once the location of a large reservoir, from where water was piped all over the island. Also worth a look is the **Palacio de Marques**, claimed to be the oldest building on the island. Once the headquarters of the island's government, it is now a German-owned tapas bar.

Sunday Market ★★★

Teguise's peace and quiet is interrupted on Sundays, when a lively market is held in Plaza San Miguel and the surrounding streets and alleyways. This is a popular excursion for visitors from the resorts in the south of the island. There are many stalls selling craft items, jewellery, ceramics, goat's-milk cheese and other local specialities. Folklore performances and demonstrations of Canarian wrestling often take place and the local restaurants do a roaring trade. The market runs between 09:00 and 14:00. There are also numerous shops and galleries in Teguise selling quality items including the *timple*, a traditional Canarian stringed instrument which is made in the town. Be prepared for chilly winds during the winter months.

Castillo de Santa Bárbara ★★

In the east, looming over Teguise, is the extinct volcano **Guanapay**, which rises to 425m (1394ft), some 135m (443ft) above the town. Perched right on the rim of the crater of the volcano is the **Castillo de Santa Bárbara**. The original structure was a watchtower built in the early 16th century by Sancho de Herrera and used to look out for pirates coming inland from the east coast. After the bloodthirsty invasion by the Berber pirate Morato Arráez in 1586, King Felipe II sent the master fortress builder **Leonardo Torriani** to strengthen the fort. Within ten years the castle was looking very much as it does today.

By the 20th century it had become rather decrepit and in 1989 the local council took responsibility for its renovation with the help of a concerted campaign by locals keen to save

GOLF ON LANZAROTE

Lanzarote is not exactly a golfers' paradise, but this may change in the future. The lack of rainfall means that it is expensive to maintain the manicured courses that golfers have come to expect. Nevertheless, Lanzarote does have one excellent golf course located on the outskirts of Costa Teguise. It has 18 holes (par 72), a driving range, a practice putting green, a restaurant, bar and pro shop. A handicap of 28 is required for men and 32 for ladies. Tolleys, buggies and clubs can be hired. A second course, known as Lanzarote Golf, has recently opened on the outskirts of Puerto del Carmen (tel: 928 514050, www.lanzarotegolfresort.com). It is an 18-hole par 72 course created by the well-known US designer Ron Kirby. There is also a pitch and putt facility in the Playa Blanca area.

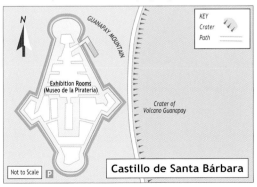

KEY
Crater
Path

Exhibition Rooms
(Museo de la Piratería)

Crater of
Volcano Guanapay

GUANAPAY MOUNTAIN

Not to Scale

Castillo de Santa Bárbara

CENTRAL LANZAROTE

COCHINEAL

The production of cochineal is one of Lanzarote's more unusual industries. Cochineal is a red dye made from the larvae of the cochineal beetle (*Cocus cacti*). The production is centred around the villages of **Guatiza** and **Mala** in the east of the island. Here you can see scores of fields growing the **prickly pear** (*Opuntia ficus-indica*) on which the cochineal beetle feeds. The beetles' larvae are collected and killed in hot water. They are then dried in the sun and crushed, resulting in a powder that forms the red dye. The industry suffered when synthetic dyes were introduced in the late 19th century, but today, with the emphasis on natural products, cochineal farming is making a comeback. Cochineal is used to colour soft drinks and it is also used in cosmetics, foods and pharmaceuticals. It is even said to provide the red colour in Campari!

this piece of history. It now houses the **Museo de la Piratería** or Museum of Piracy, charting the era when the Canary Islands were ravaged by attacks from the water.

Of course the main reason for these attacks was the vast amount of treasure returning from Spanish colonies in the New World. Pirates acted independently, but they were also 'contracted' by various European monarchies to perform acts against their enemies on lands far from their mainland power bases. The museum is open Monday–Friday 10:00–15:30, Sundays 10:30–14:30 (closed Saturdays). There is a good road from Teguise to the castle, with a small car park next to the entrance. It is possible to walk to the castle, but this is not advisable in hot weather. A rough track runs around the crater's rim and many visitors walk down into the bottom of the crater, as is shown by the number of names formed with stones.

COSTA TEGUISE AND THE EAST COAST

There are three main resorts on Lanzarote – Playa Blanca, **Costa Teguise** and Puerto del Carmen. Of these, Costa Teguise is the newest and smartest and has the distinction of having been built entirely from scratch on land that was formerly lava fields and salt pans. The work began in the late 1970s, spurred on by the opening of the luxury **Meliá Salinas Hotel**. With its central atrium, water gardens, three court-

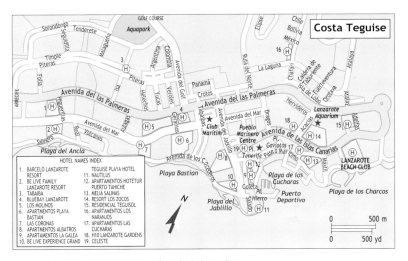

Costa Teguise

HOTEL NAMES INDEX
1. BARCELÓ LANZAROTE RESORT
2. BE LIVE FAMILY LANZAROTE RESORT
3. TABAIBA
4. BLUEBAY LANZAROTE
5. LOS MOLINOS
6. APARTMENTS PLAYA BASTIAN
7. LAS CORONAS
8. APARTMENTOS ALBATROS
9. APARTAMENTOS LA GALEA
10. BE LIVE EXPERIENCE GRAND TEGUISE PLAYA HOTEL
11. NAUTILUS
12. APARTAMENTOS HOTETUR PUERTO TAHICHE
13. MELIA SALINAS
14. RESORT LOS ZOCOS
15. RESIDENCIAL TEGUISOL
16. APARTAMENTOS LOS NARANJOS
17. APARTAMENTOS LAS CUCHARAS
18. H10 LANZAROTE GARDENS
19. CELESTE

yards of restaurants and plethora of tropical plants, it was a sensation when it opened and it remains Lanzarote's top hotel today. However, further developments in Costa Teguise were not so smooth. César Manrique had played a part in its initial planning, with the Canary-style fishing village of **Puerto Marinero** surrounded by traditional buildings. However, tourists were slow to come and the development firm went bankrupt. Construction was taken over by a company from the Spanish mainland, who relieved Manrique of his consultancy and proceeded to develop the resort in a way that many people feel is not in harmony with the original concept.

Today, Costa Teguise is still growing and will eventually be able to offer 40,000 beds for tourists. A further three hotels have been built, as well as scores of apartment blocks and villas. There are a number of commercial centres (the main one is Las Cucheras), where most of the shops, restaurants and entertainment can be found. Costa Teguise has five **beaches** of white sand. The largest of these is **Playa de las Cucharas**, which offers a full range of water sports. **Playa de los Charcos** is protected by sea walls and is the location of the Lanzarote Beach Club. A promenade runs the

◀ *Opposite: The Meliá Salinas, Lanzarote's top hotel, is located at the resort of Costa Teguise.*

CENTRAL LANZAROTE

▶ *Right: A cactus sculpture by Manrique outside his Jardín de Cactus.*

THE VIRGIN OF THE VOLCANOES

On the edge of the village of **Mancha Blanca** is a delightful little whitewashed church, with black volcanic cornerstones. This is the **Ermita de los Dolores** (The Hermitage of the Virgin of Sorrows). In 1824, the Tinguatón volcano erupted and lava flowed out towards the village of Mancha Blanca. The inhabitants prayed to the Virgin to save the village from destruction. Miraculously, thanks to the Virgin, the lava stopped at the edge of the settlement. Step inside the Ermita to see the Virgin in her position behind the altar. A pilgrimage (*romería*) proceeds to the Ermita each September, followed by the island's most important fiesta celebrating the Virgin of the Volcanoes.

length of the beaches, backed by restaurants and shops.

Costa Teguise has proved to be popular with people wishing to buy homes on Lanzarote, including royalty and a number of celebrities. Although the future of the resort is assured, potential visitors should remember that the site covers some 11km² (4.2 square miles) and many parts have a rather sterile, unfinished look. Many tourists at Costa Teguise find that a hired car is helpful to reach the various facilities at the resort.

Costa Teguise is the location of the first golf course to be built on Lanzarote, situated just northwest of the resort. Designed by John Harris, it is an 18-hole (par 72) course, with a shop, driving range, bar and restaurant. With over 3000 palm trees, the lush course contrasts strangely with the barren volcanoes and lava fields around it (tel: 928 590512, www.lanzarote-golf.com).

Aquapark *

Right next to the golf course is the **Aquapark**, which offers a full range of slides and pools, providing an ideal day out for families. The water park is open daily between 10:00 and 18:00. The park is closed November–March. Buses, free of charge, pick people up from various parts of the island.

Lanzarote Aquarium

This Costa Teguise attraction claims to be the largest aquarium in the Canary Islands. It has a huge collection of fish and includes 'touching pools' that will appeal to children. It also offers the opportunity for suitably qualified visitors to dive with sharks. Open daily 10:00–18:00 (tel: 928 590069, www.aquariumlanzarote.com).

A **Friday craft market** takes place every week in the Centro Pueblo Marinero.

GUATIZA REGION

From Costa Teguise the coastal road leads northwards and eventually reaches the towns of **Guatiza** and **Mala**, the centre of the cochineal-producing industry. Here are fields of the prickly pear cactus on which the cochineal insect feeds. If you look closely at the cacti you may see the silver-grey marks left by the beetle. Guatiza is a prosperous-looking town, with a main street lined with mature eucalyptus trees – an unusual sight in Lanzarote.

▼ *Below: There is no mistaking which toilet to enter at the Jardín de Cactus.*

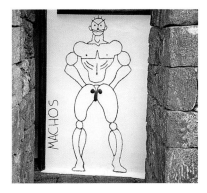

CENTRAL LANZAROTE

Jardín de Cactus ★★★

Just north of Guatiza on the right-hand side of the road is one of the island's main attractions – César Manrique's **Cactus Garden**. It is located in an old *rofero* (quarry), where local farmers dug out volcanic lapilli (*see* panel, page 101) for their fields. The garden has nearly 10,000 cacti of 1420 species brought from all over the world, but the most remarkable one is the metal sculpture by Manrique, 8m (26ft) in height, just outside the main entrance. Dominating the garden is a restored windmill, which shows clearly the way corn was ground to make *gofio*. There is also a small shop, a classy Manrique-designed restaurant, and a number of Manrique's paintings are on show in the entrance area. Don't miss the toilets with their extraordinary and amusing symbols for men and women. Open daily 10:00–17:45, tel: 928 529397; entrance fee.

▲ *Above: Just a few of the thousands of cacti in the Jardín de Cactus.*
▶ ▶ *Opposite: Wind turbines provide a useful source of energy, as Lanzarote has no fossil fuels.*

A minor road leads from Guatiza through the cactus fields to the small coastal village of **Los Cocoteros** where some development has recently occurred. There are a few abandoned salt pans here that attract wading birds during the migration season.

Los Valles

Inland from Guatiza, along the GC700 route, is the attractive village of **Los Valles**. Its full name is Los Valles de Santa Catalina, as its original residents resettled here from the village of Santa Catalina in 1730 when their homes were buried under lava from the Timanfaya eruptions. The new inhabitants have worked hard to make their adopted area productive, and the valley-side terraces have crops of beans, potatoes and barley. This is one of the best spots on the island to see people working the fields in the traditional way with the time-honoured headwear, while donkeys and camels (often harnessed together) pull farm equipment. Los Valles is also a good place to note how, in rural farming communities, the *Lanzaroteños* add new blocks and extensions to their houses when their sons and daughters get married. It is worth taking a detour northwards from Los Valles to the **Ermita de las Nieves**, a small whitewashed chapel located at 643m (2110ft) above sea level. From this quiet and windy place there are wonderful views of the Risco de Famara cliffs and the sandy plain of El Jable. Just northeast of Los Valles is the **Parque Eólico** wind farm. The public are not allowed on the premises, but it offers an excellent photo opportunity.

Fundación César Manrique ★★★

Take the LZ-1 road north out of Arrecife towards **Tahiche**. After a short distance there is a distinctive Manrique wind chime sculpture on a roundabout. Turn left here and just to the right is the Taro de Tahiche, home of the **César Manrique Foundation**, located in the house that the artist occupied from 1968 to 1987, after which he moved to a farmhouse in Haría. In 1992 his former house became the headquarters of the César Manrique Foundation and was opened as a museum. The ground floor looks like a standard example of Canarian architecture, but Manrique had always wanted to live with the lava, and the house is built over five lava

WINDMILLS AND OTHER FORMS OF ENERGY

Lanzarote has no deposits of fossil fuels such as coal, oil or natural gas. Nor can it generate electricity by using running water, owing to low precipitation levels. The rainfall is also insufficient to construct reservoirs, so desalinization plants have been built to supply drinking water. Inevitably, there has been research into renewable forms of energy. Fortunately, Lanzarote has plenty of sun and wind and it is now standard for new houses and industrial premises to have solar power. Windmills have always been used on the island to grind grain, and now the first modern wind farm has been built on the hills near Los Valles to generate electricity. Others are likely to follow.

▲ *Above: A tasteful water feature at the César Manrique Foundation.*

'bubbles' dating from the volcanic eruptions that took place between 1730 and 1736. The bubbles are linked by tunnels, and throughout there is the striking contrast between the blue-black lava and the whitewashed walls. Each of the bubbles was a separate room in the house and each was emphasized with a different colour scheme. Some are open to the sky, such as the dining room with its traditional stove. Water also plays an integral part in the design, with the pool and a tinkling fountain. In one bubble, a palm tree grows up through the roof of the lava. Back in the entrance area, at ground level, there is an art gallery which includes works by Picasso, Tapies, Miró and, of course, Manrique himself. The gallery has a huge picture window looking out over the lava fields, while outside there is a snack bar, a bookshop and a massive outdoor mural. Open daily 10:00–18:00, reduced hours in winter, entrance fee (tel: 928 843138, www.fcmanrique.org).

Few fail to be impressed by the César Manrique Foundation, and most visitors will feel the urge to see more of his imaginative projects. In fact, just 7km (4 miles) to the west and in the exact centre of the island is the **Monumento al Campesino**, a white cubist monument, some 15m (49ft) high, made from the remnants of old fishing boats and water tanks. The full name of the monument is *El Monumento*

Fecundidad al Campesino Lanzaroteño (the Fertility Monument to the *Lanzaroteño* Peasant), and Manrique dedicated the sculpture to the forgotten endeavours of the unknown farmers of Lanzarote. Look hard at the monument and with some imagination you will be able to pick out a farmer with his donkey and camel. Next to the monument is the **Casa Museo del Campesino**, a museum based on a traditional farmhouse. Here you can see the farm equipment and tools, such as ploughs and saddlery. Potters and basket-weavers display their traditional skills, while a dromedary works a mill to make the *gofio* that is served in the museum's restaurant along with other Canarian specialities. The museum is open daily between 10:00 and 18:00.

San Bartolomé

Just to the south of the Monumento al Campesino, 7km (4.3 miles) northwest of Arrecife, is the busy administrative town of **San Bartolomé**. In the central square is the parish church, the town hall and a refurbished municipal theatre. In Calle Constitución there is an **Ethnographic Museum Tanit**, located in a traditional 18th-century house that belonged to the Perdomo family. It has a comprehensive collection

THE CANARY PALM

Because of its arid climate, Lanzarote is largely treeless. An exception, however, is the **Canary palm** (*Phoenix canariensis*), which is found in some numbers in the Haría area and parts of central Lanzarote, where its is often planted to provide shade around farmhouses. It is actually a very useful tree, as the leaves are an essential raw material for the handicraft industry in the Canary Islands and they are used to make mats and baskets. Furthermore, the timber can be utilized for construction and the sap can be extracted to make palm honey. Unfortunately, in Lanzarote, the palm tree is far too valuable to chop down. Interestingly, the number of palms on the island is actually increasing as they are often planted in hotel gardens, where they make attractive landscape features.

◄ *Left: Manrique's Monumento al Campesino, made from old boats and water tanks.*

The visitor to Lanzarote can travel all round the island and never see a herd of cattle. Sheep are also rarely seen, and pigs, if they are kept at all, will spend their lives in barns. The only domestic farm animals likely to be spotted are herds of goats. It is therefore surprising to see that meat features prominently on restaurant menus, both in the tourist areas and in the inland villages. Beef (**carne de vaca**) is mainly imported from South America, while pork (**cerdo**) and lamb (**cerdero**) are brought in from other Canary Islands. Kid (**cabrito**) is a local favourite, but quite expensive. A good alternative is rabbit (**conejo**), which is usually served with *mojo* sauce. Many of the country restaurants in the centre of Lanzarote, such as the restaurant at the **Museo del Campesino** near Mozaga, will serve traditional meat dishes.

of farming equipment, household items and musical instruments showing how the island's culture has changed over the last 200 years. The museum is open from Monday to Saturday (10:00–14:00). A more modern attraction is Lanzarote's Go-Karting track, which is located just to the south of San Bartolumé on the Arrecife road. It is open from 10:00 until sunset and there is a bar and a children's playground; tel: 928 520022.

TIAGUA

North of the Monumento al Campesino roundabout the LZ-20 road passes through **Mozaga** and then arrives at **Tiagua**, where, at the crossroads, you will find the simple, but delightfully photogenic, 18th-century **Ermita de la Virgen de Perpetuo**.

Museo Agrícola El Patio ★★★

Turn right at the crossroads and head in the direction of the windmills marking the location of the **Museo Agrícola El Patio**. Most visitors are enthralled by this agricultural museum, which well deserves the prizes it has won. The main building is a manor house, which once belonged to the Count de la Quinta. In the early 20th century, this was the largest and most efficiently farmed estate in Lanzarote, employing 25 farm workers and 20 camels. By the second half of the century, with the onset of tourism, many workers had left the land and taken up other work. In 1994 the estate was converted into a museum, which has already won a tourism prize. There are actually two museums here, based on either side of a large courtyard. On the right as you enter is the old manor house, which has been retained much as it was in the early 20th century. It is possible to wander through the rooms of the house – including living rooms, bedrooms and kitchen – and out into the grape press, bodega and grain store. There is also a meeting room, small chapel, wine museum and cactus garden. There are a variety of farm animals in the courtyard, including chickens, donkeys and a dromedary. The left-hand side of the courtyard is dominated

by two restored windmills. One is the thin type made of wood, known as the female windmill, while the other is the larger plastered type with a tiled roof, known as the male windmill. It is possible to go inside both windmills and see the way in which corn was ground into *gofio*. There is also an example of an animal-driven mill. The buildings on this side of the courtyard form the main agricultural museum, with a wide collection of farming implements, harnesses and other artefacts. The tour ends at the bodega, where the local *El Patio* wine can be tasted, along with other delicacies such as goat's-milk cheese. The Museo Agrícola El Patio is open Monday to Friday (10:00–17:30) and Saturdays (10:00–14:30), entrance fee; tel: 928 529134, www.museoelpatio.com

▲ *Above: The simple Ermita de la Virgen de Perpetuo at the Tiagua crossroads.*

TINAJO REGION

From Tiagua the LZ-20 swings northwest towards a conglomeration of prosperous agricultural villages. **Tinajo** is the main administrative village of the north and it is famous for the skill of its wrestlers – look out for the arena on the road to the south of the village. The parish church of San Roque, which has a sundial dated 1881 on its roof, is also worth a look. The interior has an impressive wooden

▲ *Above: Mancha Blanca's church, the Ermita de los Dolores, was threatened by encroaching lava in 1824.*

Mudéjar ceiling and some fine statues, including one by Luján Pérez, the best-known Canarian sculptor. Linked with Tinajo, to the south, is the village of **Mancha Blanca**, famous for its church, the **Ermita de los Dolores**, and its statue, Nuestra Señora de los Volcanes. The church was built in honour of the virgin, who, it is claimed, saved the village from destruction in 1824 when the nearby volcano of Tinguatón erupted. The island's main fiesta and pilgrimage takes place here every September.

Northeast of Tinajo and south of the village of **Sóo** is the sandy plain of **El Jable**. This area is well known to bird-watchers as it is the best spot on the island to see Lanzarote's desert species, such as houbara bustard, stone curlew, cream-coloured courser and trumpeter bullfinch.

THE NORTH COAST

Generally rocky and inhospitable, the north coast has few settlements, with the notable exception of **La Santa**, a growing village sustained by the large sporting complex of **Club La Santa**. The club is able to offer facilities for 64 Olympic sports, a fact confirmed in the *Guinness Book of Records*. Professional international sportspeople flock here in the winter for warm-weather training, but there are many courses available for amateurs and families. The club has an

Olympic-sized swimming pool, an athletics stadium and an artificial lagoon specially created for beginners' courses in windsurfing and kitesurfing (tel: 928 599999, www.clublasanta.com). La Santa village benefits from the proximity of the club and has a number of thriving fish restaurants. Just to the west of the club is a low-lying peninsula known as La Isleta, which was formerly an island. A road runs all the way around **La Isleta**, providing excellent points to watch surfers and sailboarders, while a shallow inlet is attractive to migrating sea birds and waders.

Further along the coast is the only other settlement, the pretty fishing village of **La Caleta de Famara**, where César Manrique spent his childhood. There are one or two good seafood restaurants in the village. This marks the start of Lanzarote's best sandy beach, the **Playa de Famara**. Unfortunately it is plagued by strong winds and tides and is usually too dangerous for swimming, but the surfing is excellent and this is the home of Costa N-Oeste (*see* page 65), one of Lanzarote's best surfing schools. A shipwreck confirms the strength of the Famara winds. The *playa* is backed by huge cliffs called the **Risco de Famara**, which rise to over 600m (1969ft) and are a popular location for hang-gliding.

◀ *Left: Windsurfing is just one of many activities provided at La Santa Sports Centre.*

CENTRAL LANZAROTE AT A GLANCE

BEST TIMES TO VISIT
Central Lanzarote can be visited at any time of the year, but be prepared for strong winds on the north coast in the winter. In summer, the inland areas can be hot. The fiesta at Mancha Blanca, in September each year, celebrates the Virgin of the Volcanoes. It should not be missed.

GETTING THERE
Buses run from Arrecife to most of the villages of central Lanzarote (line 7), but the service is patchy. There are few links with the main resorts. **Coach** excursions only visit the main tourist locations. A hired **car** is the most convenient way to reach central Lanzarote.

GETTING AROUND
Once again, a hired **car** is essential to cover the best locations in the area. It is also the most convenient way to explore this region, as signposting and road surfaces are usually excellent and the distances involved are small. There is also a very good network of petrol stations.

WHERE TO STAY
There is little, if any, accommodation available in central Lanzarote, except in the resort of Costa Teguise. Even here there is no accommodation in the budget range. Beds in the self-catering apartments far outnumber those in hotels.

Costa Teguise
Luxury
Hotel Meliá Salinas, Avda Islas Canarias s/n, Costa Teguise, tel: 928 590040, fax: 928 590390, www.solmelia. com Adult-only beachfront hotel with atrium, many restaurants and subtropical gardens.

Mid-range
Be Live Experience Grand Teguise Playa, Avda del Jablillo s/n, Costa Teguise, tel: 928 590654, www.believe hotels.com Hotel overlooking Playa del Jablillo, with atrium and pools.
Be Live Family Lanzarote Resort, Avda del Mar s/n, Costa Teguise, tel: 928 590410, www.believe hotels.com Modern hotel next to Playa del Ancla. Excellent leisure facilities.
H10 Lanzarote Gardens, Avda Islas Canarias 13, Costa Teguise, tel: 928 590100, fax: 928 591784, www.hotel h10lanzarotegardens.com Good family aparthotel near to Las Cucharas beach.
Celeste, Avda Islas Canarias s/n, Costa Teguise, tel: 928 591720, fax: 928 592482. Centrally located apartments, close to windsurfing school.
Puerto Tahiche, Plaza de Janubio 2, Costa Teguise, tel: 928 590118, fax: 928 590117, www.hotelturtahiche.com Family-friendly, self-catering.

Rural Accommodation
The following farmhouses and small country houses can be recommended:
Casa Barranco, Los Valles, tel: 619 231904, www.rural-villas.com
Casa Catalina, Calle San Isidro Labrador 12, Los Valles, tel: 619 231904, www.rural-villas.com

WHERE TO EAT
For fresh seafood, head to La Santa and La Caleta on the north coast. A number of inland towns and villages, particularly in Teguise, serve traditional Canarian dishes. Costa Teguise has a variety of international food outlets.

Teguise
Mid-range
Acatife, Calle San Miguel 4, Teguise, tel: 928 845037. International food with a Canarian flavour in an atmospheric 18th-century house.
Ikarus, Calle Clavijo y Fajardo, Teguise, tel: 928 845332. Fine food in an old manor house with its own art gallery. Open lunchtimes and Thur–Fri evenings.
La Cantina, Calle León y Castillo 8, Teguise, tel: 928 845536, www.cantinateguise. com Spanish food and *tapas* in 18th-century palacio.

Costa Teguise
Luxury
Marea, Hotel Meliá Salinas, Costa Teguise, tel: 928 590040. Pricey international food in the island's top hotel.

Mid-range
El Pescador, Pueblo Marinero, Costa Teguise, tel: 928 590874. Interesting ambience in this harbourside restaurant.

Budget
The commercial centres at Costa Teguise, such as Las Cucharas and Las Maretas, have a range of budget outlets such as Tex-Mex, Chinese and American fast-food chains.
Chino Chu Lin, Calle Tandarena, Costa Teguise, tel: 928 592011. The best of a number of Chinese restaurants in the resort, with a takeaway service.

Guatiza
Jardín de Cactus, Guatiza, tel: 928 529397. After viewing Manrique's Cactus Garden, take a snack in the restaurant that he designed.

Mozaga
Casa Museo de Campesino, San Bartolomé, Mozaga road, near Monumento al Campesino, tel: 928 520136. Museum restaurant serving traditional Lanzarote dishes. A good place to try *gofio*.

La Santa
Mid-range
La Santa, Tinajo Road, La Santa, tel: 928 840353. Specializes in locally caught fish. Popular with locals and sporting types from Club La Santa.
La Caleta
El Risco, La Caleta,

tel: 928 528550, www.res taurantelrisco.com Excellent seafood restaurant, with Manrique connections.
Casa Ramon, Calle Callejon, La Caleta. Simple fresh seafood and paella, with great views of the Risco de Famara cliffs.

TOURS AND EXCURSIONS
There are a number of travel agents in Costa Teguise who arrange excursions to venues throughout the island. The most popular attractions in the central Lanzarote area are the water park at Costa Teguise, the town of Teguise with its Sunday market, and the Museo Agrícola El Patio at Tiagua. Another popular excursion follows 'In the Footsteps of César Manrique', calling at the Cactus Garden at Guatiza, the Fundación César Manrique, and other attractions in the north of the island linked with the great *Lanzaroteño*.

USEFUL CONTACTS
Oficina de Turismo. The main tourist information office in the area is at Avda. Islas Canarias, Costa Teguise, tel: 928 592542, www.turismo teguise.com
Windsurfing. There are two centres at Costa Teguise: Windsurfing Club La Cucharas, tel: 928 590731, www.lanzarotewindsurf.com and Windsurf Paradise, tel: 635 054110, www.wind surflanzarote.com

Diving at Costa Teguise can be arranged by one of the following companies: Calipso Diving, tel: 928 590879, www.calipso-diving. com and Diving Lanzarote, tel: 928 590407, www.diving lanzarote.com
Golf: Avenida de Golf s/n, 35508 Costa Teguise, tel: 928 590512, www. lanzarote-golf.com

ENTERTAINMENT
There is not very much on offer in the way of nightlife in central Lanzarote, apart from at Costa Teguise. Here, music bars include **Saxos**, while **Treble** is a lively sports bar. For karaoke, head to **Jester's** just off Pueblo Marinero. The **Lively Lady Show Bar** on Avenida de Islas Canarias has regular drag cabaret performances.

SHOPPING
Most of the villages in central Lanzarote have shops selling locally made basketwork, embroidery, pottery and jewellery. The **César Manrique Foundation** has an outlet at La Lonja, Plaza 18 de Julio, Teguise. Don't miss the **Sunday market** in the centre of Teguise, where a number of stalls sell craft items. Souvenirs can also be bought at the shops in the commercial centres at Costa Teguise, such as Las Maretas and Las Cucharas.

5 Southern Lanzarote and Timanfaya National Park

Southern Lanzarote, an area of contrasting features and extremely varied landscape, is dominated by the **Timanfaya National Park** containing over 30 volcanic cones within its boundary – this is every visitor's favourite excursion. These same volcanoes left vast areas of lava flows, with their dark jagged surfaces, which are known as *malpaís* or badlands. Despite the fact that they were formed over 250 years ago, these lava flows have little plant life because of Lanzarote's arid climate. South of the lava field lies the flat gravel plain of **El Rubicón**, which is almost totally devoid of vegetation. In contrast, fine crops of grapes are grown in volcanic granules called *picón* in the fertile valley of **La Geria**. The coastline is also varied; **Papagayo** in the south is typified by sandy beaches while in the north, at **Los Hervideros**, the Atlantic waves have etched out the lava cliffs into strange shapes and nearby, at **El Golfo**, the waves have eaten into the cone of a volcano, exposing layers of ash and lava, leaving a strange green lake in the crater floor.

SOUTHERN LANZAROTE

The south of the island is home to two of Lanzarote's main tourist resorts, but they are very different in character. Lively **Puerto del Carmen** stretches for 5km (3 miles) along the coast, with three magnificent beaches and all the trappings of a major resort. **Playa Blanca**, near the southern tip of the island, appeals to those who are looking for a quiet holiday. The south also has some attractive villages, with **Yaiza** often

DON'T MISS

*** Timanfaya National Park: the moon-like landscape of the 'Mountains of Fire' is a must for any visitor.
** El Golfo: a volcanic crater eroded by the sea, leaving a bright green lagoon.
** Los Hervideros: waves eroding the volcanic cliffs into cave arches and stacks.
** Beaches: The best beaches are in the south of the island.
** La Geria: see vines grown in volcanic *picón*.
* Femés: a village on a hill with stunning views.

◄ *Opposite: El Diablo (the Devil) makes an apt logo for Timanfaya National Park.*

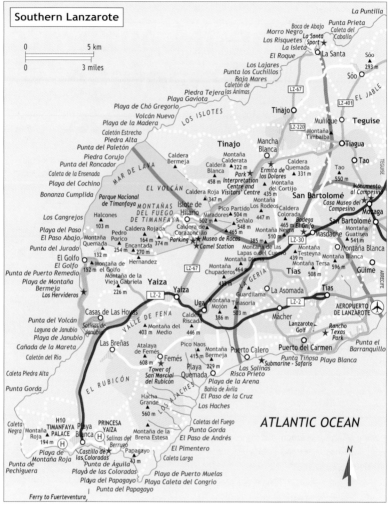

winning awards for its picture-postcard beauty. **El Golfo** is noted for its fish restaurants and its sunsets, while **Puerto Calero**'s photogenic harbour has the best collection of yachts on the island. Don't miss little **Femés**, perched high up in the mountains, providing some of the best views on Lanzarote.

Puerto del Carmen

Just ten minutes from Arrecife Airport in the municipality of Tías is Puerto del Carmen, Lanzarote's major resort, accommodating 60 per cent of the island's visitors and providing 30,000 beds in apartments and hotels. Puerto del Carmen stretches in a narrow ribbon along 5km (3 miles) of coast and includes three large sandy beaches. Despite its size, there are no high-rise structures and it is essentially a pleasant place to stay.

The Harbour

The old part of Puerto del Carmen is in the west and based around the old harbour. This was the original settlement, once known as **La Tiñosa**, a tiny fishing village. The harbour still has its fishing boats, now joined by a variety of other craft, such as diving boats, launches, ferries and fishing boats for deep-sea sports. Next to the harbour is an adventure playground backed by a series of restaurants specializing in seafood.

East of the harbour, the picture changes. A long road, the **Avenida de las Playas**, forms a busy seaside strip. On one side is a promenade, rich in palms and colourful subtropical plants. The other side of the *avenida* consists of shops, restaurants, bars and amusement arcades. It is said that there are over 200 restaurants in Puerto del Carmen and at least half of them are located along Avenida de las Playas. They include Indian, Chinese, Tex-Mex, Italian and just about every other type of cuisine you can imagine. Add to this list sports bars, English pubs, Irish bars and German beer gardens. Nightlife is around the various commercial centres, such as **Centro Atlántico** and **Biosfera Plaza**, with their nightclubs and discos. Further east the *avenida* becomes progressively quieter, with tasteful *urbanizaciónes* (housing estates), apartments and the occasional hotel.

Beaches ★★

Puerto del Carmen has three superb sandy beaches. The most westerly, and the busiest, is **Playa Grande** (also known, confusingly, as Playa Blanca – the same name given to the

---

TIMESHARE TOUTS

One of the irritations of a holiday in Puerto del Carmen is the ubiquitous timeshare tout, who hangs around the promenade and other crowded places. Officially known as an off-property contact, his job is to entice visitors, with ploys such as free gifts and holiday offers, to go to a timeshare location. Here, hard-sell techniques are employed. The idea is to persuade visitors to buy a share in a property in which they can take a holiday for one or two weeks a year for life. For some people the idea is attractive, but for many, especially those who like to visit a variety of holiday spots or enjoy staying in hotels, it is unsuitable. The best advice is to have a cooling-off period during which you can change your mind, and not to sign anything until you are absolutely sure of the financial implications.

Lanzarote's main resorts – Costa Teguise, Puerto del Carmen, Playa Blanca and Puerto Calero – offer just about every conceivable type of water sport, ranging from fun craft such as pedaloes and banana boats to parascending and jet-skiing, as well as more skilful activities such as sailing, scuba diving, surfing, water-skiing and windsurfing. All water sports can be dangerous and those who take part should be aware of underwater rocks and strong currents. Do not underestimate the strength of the prevailing winds, which are at their strongest on summer afternoons and can cause problems for novices in many of the water sports.

resort further south in the island). The town's tourist office can be found alongside the beach. Past the Punta el Barranquillo is the **Playa de los Pocillos**. Finally, at the eastern end of the town is the **Playa de Matagorda**. This beach is close to the airport and suffers from a degree of aircraft noise. All the beaches offer facilities, such as chair beds and sun shades, and there are a number of *chiringuitos* (beach bars). The beaches are family-friendly and generally safe for swimming. Water sports are also available here, such as windsurfing and water-skiing, while jet-skis and pedaloes can be hired. An interesting feature of some of the town's beaches are the semicircular wind shelters made of stone, which are identical to the walls in the wine-growing areas in many parts of the island.

Just outside Puerto del Carmen is the **Rancho Texas Park**. It provides a good day out for children of all ages, its attractions including water rides, Wild West shows, a wide range of exotic animals and a mock-up of a gold mine. There are also night shows appealing more to adults. Open daily 09:30–17:30 (tel: 928 516897, www.ranchotexaslanzarote.com).

Puerto Calero

Approximately 5km (3 miles) to the west of Puerto del Carmen is the growing sport harbour of Puerto Calero. The entrance to the harbour is marked by a 12m (39ft) long skeleton of a Bryde's Whale, a cetacean that can be seen in Canarian waters from April to October, when it feeds on shoals of mackerel and sardines.

The port, which has berths for over 400 boats, is flanked by chandlers' shops, bars and restaurants. It's one of the most up-market settings in the Canary Islands with several berths for 'super-yachts' and a range of smart on-land services to match. A wide range of water activities are on offer, including

▼ *Below: Playa de los Pocillos, one of two popular beaches at the eastern end of Puerto del Carmen.*

Puerto del Carmen

catamaran sailing, sport fishing, whale and dolphin watching and submarine safaris. Amongst attractions based at Puerto Calero are the **Submarine Safaris**, offering genuine under water safaris (tel: 928 512898, www.submarinesafaris.com), and **Catlanza**, a catamaran providing an all-day sailing experience, with optional swimming, snorkelling, jet-skiing and the possibility of encountering dolphins (tel: 928 513022, www.catlanza.com).

Inland Villages

Just 5km (3 miles) inland from Puerto del Carmen is the administrative centre of **Tías**. It is a sizeable village with nearly 11,000 inhabitants, making it the second-largest settlement on the island after Arrecife. However, there is little to interest the tourist, apart from the parish church of Nuestra Señora de la Candelaria, which has a curious double belfry. The church is the centre of the fiesta activities that take place in Tías every February. Further west is another administrative centre, **Yaiza**. Part of this village was destroyed by lava flows during the Timanfaya eruptions in the 18th century. Today, Yaiza is an attractive place with some expensive and dignified houses with flower-filled gardens. Palm trees line all the roads leading into the village, and the recent building of a bypass has increased the air of tranquillity in the settlement, which was a favourite of César Manrique. Head for the central square, which is the location of the parish church, the **Iglesia Nuestra Señora de Los Remedios**. Built in the late 17th century, it has been extensively restored in recent years. The interior has a

CLIMATE

The south of Lanzarote is the driest and sunniest part of the island. It also has less wind than the north. Average January temperatures are 18°C (64°F), rising in July to 25°C (77°F). Rainfall is low, and January and October are the wettest months. Be prepared for chilly winds during the winter months in Timanfaya National Park.

THE *ENARENADO* SYSTEM

The *enarenado* system of cultivation – using volcanic *picón* as soil and semicircular walls as shelters – is well known on Lanzarote. The system has been adapted in a number of ways for other uses, such as the growing of exotic shrubs on hotel grounds. More unusual are the semicircular stone walls used as wind shelters on some of the beaches in Puerto del Carmen, and at the golf driving range on former farmland just outside the resort, where golfers aim to hit golf balls into the stone walls and hollows of *picón*.

painted wooden ceiling supported by black pillars of volcanic rock. There is also some fine carving on the gallery and altarpiece. Opposite the church is the **Benito Armas Cultural Centre**, named after the politician who lived here for over 60 years. Yaiza also has a number of craft shops and art galleries, the best known of which is the German-run **Galería Yaiza**.

On the opposite side of the bypass is Yaiza's sister village, **Uga**, which is located at the entrance of the valley of La Geria. Uga's main claim to fame is that it is the place where the camels which take tourists around the Timanfaya National Park are bred. The camels can often be seen walking along the path through the lava fields to the camel station.

Femés *

Until quite recently, the tiny village of Femés was one of Lanzarote's best-kept secrets. Nowadays it receives many visitors. It is perched on a col – at a height of 450m (1476ft) – in the mountain range known as **Los Ajaches**. It can be approached via Uga and Yaiza and this route passes through a fertile upland farming area. Look out for the house on the

LANZAROTE WINES

All of the Canary Islands produce some wine, but the quality of Lanzarote's *vino* is the finest. Known as *malvasía*, it was well known to Shakespeare who referred to it as 'sack' or 'malmsey'. The *malvasía* grape was brought to Lanzarote from Crete and it produces a wine that is famous for its strength. Red (*tinto*), rosé (*rosado*), and sweet white (*moscatel*) are all produced here and can be bought in local supermarkets. Hotels always offer Lanzarote wines in their restaurants, although it is usually more expensive than the wine from the mainland.

right-hand side with a garden full of remarkable objects, including a redundant military helicopter! In the centre of Femés is a charming little palm-lined square containing the whitewashed **Church of San Marcial del Rubicón**. The church was completed in 1733 (coincidentally when the Timanfaya eruptions were at their height) and was once the seat of a bishop. It replaced an earlier church that had been destroyed by pirates during the previous century. The interior of the church has a collection of model ships, but unfortunately the door is usually well and truly locked and only opened at the time of services. At the far end of the village square is a terrace known as the **Balcón de Femés**, providing superb views over the barren plain of **El Rubicón** and down towards Playa Blanca, with Fuerteventura in the distance. This is a great place to watch sunsets, particularly if you are having an evening meal at one of the two excellent restaurants in Femés. A clear hiking trail leads from the village to the summit of **Atalaya de Femés**, which rises to 608m (1995ft) and offers even more spectacular views. There is an alternative, steeper route down to Playa Blanca, via Las Breñas, which passes en route some *picón* quarries.

La Geria ★★

The LZ-30 road runs northeast from **Uga** for 15km (9.3 miles) to **Masdache**, through a wine-producing area known as **La Geria**. It lies on the edge of the *malpaís* and is covered with black volcanic *picón*. Semicircular stone walls known as *zocos* shelter vines from the drying northerly winds, and plants grow in the bottom of funnel-shaped hollows; there are reckoned to be over 10,000 of these *zocos* on the island. The wine-producing area covers over 3000ha (7413 acres) and has become quite a popular tourist attraction. The *malvasía* wine that is produced here can be sampled at a number of bodegas. **Bodega La Geria**, which also has a gift shop, is a favourite stop for coaches. **Bodega El Chupadero**, some 4km (2.5 miles) north of Uga, is just off the main road and you can sample wine more peacefully here. Further north, in Masdache, is **Bodega El Campesino**. On the out-

◄ *Opposite: The dignified main square of Yaiza is backed by the 17th-century parish church.*

DRY FARMING

On an island famed for its unusual landscapes, the most remarkable is found in the valley of La Geria. Here vines are grown by the **enarenado** method. They are planted in hollows, in the black granules of volcanic ash called *picón,* and sheltered by low semi-circular stone walls. The *picóns* act as hard sponges and store any rain that falls. They also trap any dew that collects, particularly on clear nights. The *Lanzaroteños* formerly used sand for this dry-farming process, but discovered – after the eruptions of the early 18th century – that *picón* was a far better water-holding material. So successful is the *enarenado* method that some vines can produce as many as 200kg (441lb) of grapes.

skirts of Masdache is the oldest of the bodegas, **El Grifo**, which was founded in 1775. It is generally accepted that this bodega makes the best wine on the island and it is available in all the top restaurants. El Grifo also has a small **wine museum**, which shows how wine-making equipment has changed over the years. The museum is open daily (10:30–18:00).

Wine tours are available at all of the bodegas, but book in advance and make sure that the tour is in the language of your choice.

Coastal Erosion on the North Coast ★★

When the lava spread out from the volcanoes in the eruptions of the early 18th century, it not only covered villages and fertile farmland but also flowed into the sea, considerably increasing the land area of Lanzarote. Ever since then the Atlantic Ocean has been doing its best to claim the land back. At **El Golfo**, the sea has eroded away a volcano, exposing the wall of the crater and displaying a marvellous cross-section of lava and ash in a variety of colours. Beneath the crater wall is a halfmoon-shaped lake called **Lago Verde** on account of its bright green colour that is caused by the micro-organisms, which are believed to be unique to this lake. Between the lake and the ocean is a beach of black volcanic

▶ *Right: At Los Hervideros on the west coast, the waves of the Atlantic have eroded the lava flow into strange shapes.*

pebble that is as good a place as any to search for specimens of the green mineral called peridot, which is a light green glassy form of olivine. El Golfo can be approached from the south by a road leading to a small car park. Coach parties usually come from the north along a narrow path that leads to a viewing platform. This is close to the quiet village of El Golfo, which has a few fishing boats hauled up on the beach. There are half a dozen excellent fish restaurants here, many with terraces overlooking the sea and providing one of the best spots on the island to watch the sunset.

To the south of El Golfo, the road follows a dramatic stretch of coastline. To the left is Montaña Bermeja, a rusty red extinct volcano, while on the right, the sea crashes against the volcanic cliffs and seeks out the rocks' weaknesses in order to create stacks, arches and caves. The best place to view the action is at **Los Hervideros**, which literally means 'boiling waters'. From a convenient car park on the seaward side of the road, paths lead along the cliff top, giving viewing points to see the Atlantic waves crashing into the lava caves and arches. Choose a day when a heavy Atlantic swell is rolling in and you will be rewarded with the experience of pounding spray being sent metres into the air with a thunderous noise. Look out, too, for the bright red crabs that live on the rock faces in the spray zone above the waves.

▲ *Above: Lago Verde, a green-coloured lake in the breached volcano at El Golfo.*

COASTAL EROSION

Although the rock that forms volcanic cliffs is usually hard, it has many lines of weakness, such as faults and lava tubes, which can be attacked by the waves. The sheer **hydraulic force** of a wave can break open a rock face, but the shingle and sand contained in a breaking wave can wear away a rock face by **abrasion**. This results in the formation of **caves**, which later leads to erosive features such as **sea stacks** and **arches**. All of these examples can be seen in the **Los Hervideros** area in southwest Lanzarote.

SOUTHERN LANZAROTE AND TIMANFAYA NATIONAL PARK

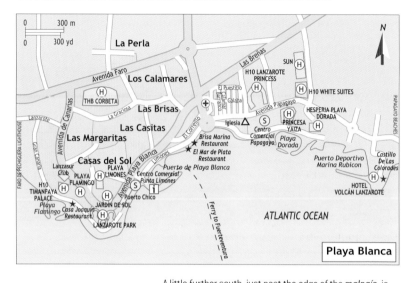

A little further south, just past the edge of the *malpaís*, is a large salt-water lagoon, the **Laguna de Janubio**. On its land- ward side are the **Salinas de Janubio**, the only commercial saltworks still operating on the island, although in a much reduced capacity. At one time the salinas produced 350,000 tons of sea salt a year, but this is now down to about 10,000 tons, as refrigerators have replaced the need to use salt in order to preserve fish. The salt pans are laid out in a chequer- board pattern, with each pan having a slightly different colour, depending on the amount of water in it. The water was once moved around by power from small windmills, but today elec- tricity is used. The salinas are a good bird-watching location, particularly in the spring and autumn, when migrant waders find the habitat attractive. South of the salinas, two parallel roads cross the barren gravel plain of **El Rubicón** en route to the southern tip of the island and the resort of Playa Blanca.

Playa Blanca

Of Lanzarote's three main resorts, Playa Blanca is the small- est and most tranquil. Once a tiny fishing port, consisting of a few houses to the east of the harbour, it has grown beyond recognition over the last 20 years, but still retains its charm. There is a small beach to the east of the harbour, but this is entirely inadequate considering the numbers that visit Playa Blanca. Fortunately two artificial beaches have been constructed. To the west of the town is the delightful little **Playa Flamingo**, sheltered by two jetties and backed by attractive subtropical gardens. This is a perfect family beach with very safe bathing. The beach was devastated by a severe and unusual storm in 2006, when the jetties were wrecked and most of the sand washed away. However the beach and facilities have been fully restored, and there's no outward sign that this weird weather event ever took place. At the other end of Playa Blanca is the expansive **Playa Dorada**, with sunbeds, sunshades and beach bars, backed by restaurants and shops. A promenade links the beaches, while just inland, parallel to the waterfront, is a part-pedestrianized street lined with shops and opening out onto a square in the east where we find the town's parish church. Just beyond Playa Dorada is the new **Rubicón Marina**, graced by expensive yachts, boardwalks and water features, while pricey shops form a backdrop.

DEEP-SEA FISHING

Visitors wishing to try their hand at deep-sea game fishing have plenty of opportunity in the south of Lanzarote. The marinas and harbours – at Puerto del Carmen, Puerto Calero and Playa Blanca – all have boats for hire, including all the necessary equipment, for small groups of anglers. The usual fish caught include marlin, swordfish, bonito and tuna. Some boats specialize in shark fishing. Book early to avoid disappointment.

▼ Below: A ferry leaves Playa Blanca harbour bound for Fuerteventura, which can be seen in the distance.

SOUTHERN LANZAROTE AND TIMANFAYA NATIONAL PARK

NUDE SUNBATHING

Topless sunbathing in Lanzarote is common on beaches and around hotel and apartment pools. Full nudity, however, is offensive to *Canarios*. There are, nevertheless, beaches where nudity is tolerated. The best-known location in Lanzarote is the **Papagayo** beach area, just to the east of Playa Blanca. Before you rush to strip off though, remember to apply plenty of protection to those areas that do not normally see the sun!

Playa Blanca's harbour is a busy ferry port, with the Fred Olsen Line and Naviera Armas operating hourly car ferry services to Corralejo on the island of Fuerteventura, which can usually be seen clearly in the distance. Other craft in the harbour include game-fishing boats, 'submarines' for underwater viewing, and diving-school craft.

There are plenty of walking options around Playa Blanca. Follow the promenade westwards and then take the paths that lead to the lighthouse, the **Faro de Pechiguera**, on the point of the same name. There are actually two lighthouses here – a low older structure and a tall new one. The more recent version was built at the prompting of César Manrique, who planned to have several of these around the shores of Lanzarote. However, the plan never came to fruition, presumably because it was too expensive. As a result of recent building developments it is now possible to reach the lighthouse by car.

A gentle walk eastwards along the promenade eventually leads to the **Castillo de las Coloradas**. It is believed that there was originally a small 15th-century castle on the same site, probably built by Jean de Béthencourt, but this was quickly destroyed by pirates. The present castle has a plaque dating its construction as 1769. It is possible to

▼ *Below: An extinct volcano, Montaña Roja, forms a backdrop to the coastal promenade at Playa Blanca.*

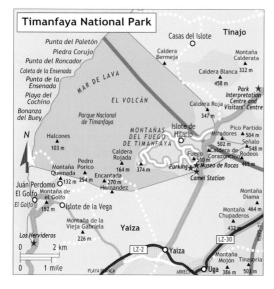

Timanfaya National Park

Punta del Paletón
Piedra Corujo
Punta del Roncador
Caleta de la Ensenada
Punta de la Ensenada
Playa del Cochino
Bonanza del Buey

MAR DE LAVA

EL VOLCÁN

Parque Nacional de Timanfaya

Casas del Islote
Tinajo

Caldera Bermeja ▲
Montaña Calderata ▲ 322 m
Caldera Blanca ▲ 458 m

Park Interpretation Centre and Visitors' Centre ★
Caldera Roja ▲ 347 m

MONTAÑAS DEL FUEGO DE TIMANFAYA

Islote de Hilario ○

N

Halcones ▲ 103 m

Pedro Porico ▲ 254 m
Montaña Quemada ▲ 164 m

Caldera Rojada ▲ 374 m

Encantada ▲ 270 m
Hernandez

Pico Partido ▲ 504 m
Miradores ▲ 502 m
Señalo ▲ 548 m
Caldera de Rodeos ▲ 465 m
Corazoncillo
Fuego ▲ 510 m

Parking ★ Museo de Rocas ★
Camel Station

Juán Perdomo ○ 132 m
El Golfo ○
El Golfo ▲ 152 m
Montaña de el Golfo
○ Islote de la Vega

Montaña de la Vieja Gabriela ▲ 226 m

Yaiza

Montaña Diama ▲
Montaña Chupaderos ▲ 464 m ▲ 432 m

Los Hervideros ★

0 _____ 2 km
0 _____ 1 mile

LZ-2 ○ Yaiza

PLAYA BLANCA

ARRECIFE ○ Uga

Montaña Mojón ▲ 386 m
Tinasoria ▲ 503 m

LZ-30

LZ(0) X2

continue walking through building sites and rough tracks to the **Papagayo beaches**, although they are more easily reached by car or boat. Papagayo consists of a series of six beaches with pale gold sand, which are considered to be some of the best in the Canary Islands. They are popular with naturists, snorkellers and surfers. Since there is absolutely no shade and very few facilities on the Papagayo beaches, come prepared with your food, enough water and a sun-shade. A launch, *Cesar II*, runs at regular intervals between Playa Blanca and Papagayo, calling at Marina Rubicón en route. This makes a pleasant excursion, even if you do not wish to land at Papagayo.

However pleasant and charming Playa Blanca seems today, its charm may not last. At the time of writing, the resort was surrounded by building sites and a forest of construction cranes. Roads, street lighting and other services have already been laid out, and it is not too far-fetched to envisage Playa Blanca stretching from the Papagayo beaches in the east to the Pechiguera lighthouse in the west. Hopefully, the buildings will be tasteful, low-rise and in traditional Canarian style.

VOLCANIC MATERIAL

Lanzarote has a long history of volcanic eruptions and almost every type of rock found on the island is of volcanic origin. The hot liquid material within a volcano is called **magma**. When the volcano erupts the magma is thrown out and it can take a number of forms. The liquid material is known as **lava** and it can flow for long distances. Explosive activity creates **ash**, which can form thick layers, and some of the ash is coarse and known as **lapilli** or *picón*, which is quite common in Lanzarote.

SOUTHERN LANZAROTE AND TIMANFAYA NATIONAL PARK

When molten **magma** erupts from a volcano, the eventual form of the lava depends on a number of factors including its chemical composition and rate of cooling. The descriptive names that are given are often Hawaiian in origin, for it was in these islands that the first research was carried out. **Aa** (pronounced 'ah-ah') is viscous material that cools quickly and has a dark, clinker-like appearance. This is the most common type of lava on Lanzarote. **Pahoehoe** (pronounced 'perhoyhoy') lava is glassier and lighter in colour and often cools as **ropey lava**. Some lava solidifies in the form of **pillows**, particularly after contact with water. **Basalt** is a fluid, black lava that travels for long distances and cools in hexagonal columns.

TIMANFAYA NATIONAL PARK

The Timanfaya area was declared one of Spain's fifteen national parks in 1974. Four of these are in the Canary Islands. The park stretches from just north of Yaiza to Mazdache and westwards and covers a sizeable length of the northwest coast – an area of almost 52km^2 (20 square miles). Unlike most national parks in the world, Timanfaya is almost completely lacking in bird, animal and plant life. Instead, visitors see a barren, but colourful, volcanic landscape, as many would imagine the surface of the moon. The park gets its name from the village of Timanfaya, one of ten settlements buried by lava and ash during the volcanic eruptions that occurred between 1730 and 1736.

Fortunately, we have an eyewitness account of the eruptions. Andrés Lorenzo Curbelo was the village priest at Yaiza at the time and he recorded the events in detail. He describes how the eruptions began in September 1730 and continued for six years. From 26 eruptions, lava and ash covered a large area of what was the most fertile farm land on the island, inundating villages and hamlets and flowing into the sea, which proceeded to boil. Curbelo describes how this resulted in thousands of dead fish, many species of which had never been seen before. Although 150km^2 (58 square miles) of land was devastated, nobody is believed to have died in the eruptions, as they managed to flee to the north of Lanzarote or to other Canary Islands.

Over 30 new volcanic cones were formed and large areas of black lava or coarse ash granules – known as lapilli or *picón* – were deposited as a result of the eruptions. These materials formed badlands or *malpaís*, and nearly 300 years after the eruptions they are still largely devoid of vegetation.

◄ Opposite: Dromedaries transport visitors over the barren volcanic slopes in Timanfaya National Park.

Visiting the Parque Nacional de Timanfaya ★★★

If holiday-makers have only time for one excursion while in Lanzarote, then it must be a trip to the Timanfaya National Park. Although most people take a coach excursion, it is possible to use a car, although this will involve transferring to one of the park's buses at some stage. Remember that roaming at will through the park is not allowed.

As you approach from Yaiza, the boundary of the park is marked by the 'fire-devil' sign at the side of the road. Shortly after this, on the left-hand side of the road, there is a car park marking the **camel station**. Here, over 100 dromedaries take visitors for a 20-minute ride over the volcanic slopes. Passengers sit in wooden seats on either side of the single hump, and it is important that the passengers are equally balanced, so the *camelleros* (dromedary handlers) use small sandbags to weigh down children or light adults. Hang on tight when the dromedary gets to its feet, as the seat will lurch forward. The camel station has a small café, toilets and a **museum** devoted to the history of the camel in Lanzarote, showing artefacts such as saddles and agricultural items used by the camels. Free entrance, open 09:00–15:00 daily.

A few kilometres further along the road an entrance fee has to be paid at a barrier. A road leads on for 2km (1.2 miles) to a hill known as the **Islote de Hilario**. *Islote* means an island of rock protruding above the surrounding lava, while Hilario is believed to have been a hermit who lived here for 50 years, accompanied only by his donkey. Crowning the hill is the **El Diablo Restaurant**, which was designed by César

COLOURFUL VOLCANIC ROCKS

Many visitors to the Timanfaya National Park are fascinated by the variety of colours seen in volcanic rocks. Generally speaking, volcanic material becomes lighter with age, so that the more recent rocks of Lanzarote are still bright with colour. Most volcanic rocks owe their colours to their **mineral content**. **Copper** produces green and blue tints, while **iron** stains rocks brown and red. Many volcanoes in Lanzarote are named after their colours, such as **Montaña Roja** (red), near Playa Blanca, **Montaña Bermeja** (orange ochre), close to El Golfo, and **Montaña Negra** (black) at Masdache. A common pale green mineral found in the lava of Lanzarote is **olivine** (the gem variety is called **peridot**) and chunks of this mineral are sold in shops.

SOUTHERN LANZAROTE AND TIMANFAYA NATIONAL PARK

Manrique as a glass-walled circle and gives superb views over the volcanic landscape westwards towards the sea. Much of the restaurant's food is grilled over a barbecue using natural heat from underground. The heat of the land below the surface is also demonstrated by the park's employees in a series of tricks; granules of hot *picón* are handed around (and very soon dropped), brushwood is placed in holes in the ground and then bursts into flames and, most spectacularly, water is poured into tubes set in the earth and erupts as steam, which shoots several metres into the sky like a man-made geyser. It is not surprising to learn that 6m (20ft) below the ground the temperature is 400°C (752°F)!

Visitors are now taken on a spectacular bus tour around the **Ruta de los Volcanes**, covering 10km (6.2 miles) and lasting about 40 minutes. The moon-like landscape is surprisingly colourful and it is possible to look down into craters, see dunes of *picón* and look into lava tubes. At one point the road passes through the steep walls of a collapsed tube. Unfortunately, although stops are made, it is not possible to get out of the bus, so photographs have to be taken through the windows.

▶▶ *Opposite: The dramatic volcanoes of Timanfaya National Park.*
▶ *Right: Lunch at El Diablo Restaurant is cooked using the residual heat of the volcano.*

The park is open daily 09:00–17:45, with the last tour at 17:00. The entry fee includes the bus tour.

If by now you are hooked on vulcanology, then pay a visit to the park's **Visitors' Centre** (the Centro de Visitantes e Interpretación de Mancha Blanca), open daily 09:00–17:00. This is located a few kilometres north – on the outskirts of the village of Mancha Blanca. The building is on the left-hand side of the road and right in the middle of the lava fields. The museum was opened in 1996 and it is full of hi-tech equipment which demonstrates the working of volcanoes. Large windows look out onto the lava, with volcanoes in the background to give immediate and practical examples of the theory being explained. As well as geology, there are also displays of the natural and social history of Lanzarote. There are audiovisual demonstrations at regular intervals. Children enjoy the visit to the bowels of the centre where a simulated eruption may be experienced, complete with colour, noise and smoke! You can also follow boardwalks out onto the lower fields.

The Visitors' Centre is also the only place where you can book guided hiking trips in the park. There are two walks on offer. One goes around the central volcanoes, while the other follows the northwest coast. Both are demanding – hikers should be fit and well equipped. The walks are very popular and usually fully booked several days in advance.

LONG-DISTANCE MIGRANTS

Butterflies are not particularly common in Lanzarote, largely owing to the lack of flowers and nectar on which they feed. However, two species that are often found in hotel grounds are the **monarch** (*Danaus plexippus*) and the **painted lady** (*Cynthia cardui*). While both species are resident and breed in the Canary Islands, they also undertake lengthy migrations northwards. The monarch is occasionally seen in the coastal parts of France and Holland, while the painted lady can often be seen in huge numbers all over northern Europe. In Britain, the painted lady can have two broods in favourable years, but it is unable to survive the northern European winters. Surprisingly, the monarch and the painted lady are often seen migrating northwards together.

SOUTHERN LANZAROTE AND TIMANFAYA NATIONAL PARK AT A GLANCE

BEST TIMES TO VISIT
The south is the driest, sunniest and least windy – a good place to be in winter. Jul–Aug can be hot, particularly if the sirocco wind is blowing. Be prepared for chilly winds if visiting the Timanfaya National Park in winter.

GETTING THERE
Regular buses go from Arrecife to Puerto del Carmen (route 2), and Arrecife to Playa Blanca (route 60), but not to the Timanfaya National Park.

GETTING AROUND
Bus service to smaller towns and villages is patchy – hire a car to reach remote locations. Roads and signposting are good, so navigating in the area is not a problem.

WHERE TO STAY
There are no *pensiónes* in the south and therefore no budget accommodation. Almost all accommodation in the south is at the resorts of Puerto del Carmen and Playa Blanca.

Puerto del Carmen
Luxury
Hotel Los Fariones, Roque del Este 1, Puerto del Carmen, tel: 928 510175, fax: 928 515200, www.farioneshotels.com Dating from 1966, this traditional hotel in subtropical gardens provides every comfort.
Hotel Jameos Playa, Playa de los Pocillos, Puerto del Carmen, tel: 928 511717, fax:

928 514219, www.los-jameos-playa.co.uk Beachside hotel with excellent sports facilities.

Mid-range
Hipotel La Geria, Calle Jupiter 5, Playa de los Pocillos, Puerto del Carmen, tel: 928 510441, fax: 928 511919, www.hipotels.com Seafront hotel; good leisure facilities.
VIK Hotel San Antonio, Avda. de las Playas 84, Puerto del Carmen, tel: 928 514200, fax: 928 513080, www.vikhotels.com Older hotel with gardens, good facilities.

Playa Blanca
Luxury
Princesa Yaiza, Avda Papaguyo 22, tel: 928 519300, www.princesayaiza.com This luxury Canarian-style hotel's facilities include six restaurants, park and health and sports centres.
Hotel Volcán Lanzarote, Calle El Castillo 1, Playa Blanca 35570, tel: 928 519185, www.hotelvolcanlanzarote.com Luxury hotel close to the marina, built in the shape of a volcano. The entrance area is a replica of the interior of Teguise parish church.

Mid-range
Hotel Lanzarote Park, Urb. Montaña Roja, Playa Blanca 35570, tel: 928 517084, fax: 928 517348, www.iberostar.com Comfortable, good leisure facilities next to beach.
H10 Lanzarote Princess, Calle Maciot s/n, Playa Blanca 35570, tel: 928 517108, fax:

928 517011, www.hotelh10lanzaroteprincess.com Large comfortable child-friendly hotel, set back from the town centre.
Hotel Timanfaya Palace, Urb. Montaña Roja 27, Playa Blanca 35570, tel: 928 517676, fax: 928 517035, www.hotelh10timanfayapalace.com Seafront hotel with impressive atrium, subtropical gardens.

Rural Accommodation
Finca de las Salinas, Calle la Cuesta 17, Yaiza, tel: 928 830325, fax: 928 830329. Based on an 18th-century mansion.
Casa Diama, la Gería, tel: 928 800663, www.casadiama.com Country house in the wine-producing valley.
La Finca Uga, Calle Agachadilla 5, Uga, tel: 629 372220, www.fincauga.com Farmhouse on the edge of the *malpaís*.

WHERE TO EAT
Restaurants to suit every taste and pocket can be found in Lanzarote's chief resort of Puerto del Carmen, where there are over 200 establishments. There is also a good selection in Playa Blanca, and some fine country restaurants serving traditional Canarian food in the inland villages of Uga, Yaiza and Femés. For the freshest seafood, head for the coastal village of El Golfo.

Puerto del Carmen
Mid-range
El Sardinero, Calle Nuestra

Señora del Carmen 9, Puerto del Carmen, tel: 928 511933. Highly regarded seafood restaurant near the harbour.
La Cañada, Calle César Manrique 3, Puerto del Carmen, tel: 928 501415. Worth visiting for this rare example of typical Canarian food.
Bozena's, Calle Teide 6, tel: 928 511463, www.bozenas-restaurant.com Specialises in Polish and international dishes.
Casa Cabana, Calle Teide 9, tel: 626 724713, www.casacabanalanzarote.co.uk Wide range of freshly cooked British and continental dishes.
Las Vegas, Avenida de las Playas, tel: 928 513346. Contemporary menu presented with style and excellent service.

Budget
Zaffran, Calle Juan Carlos 1, tel: 928 512747, www.zaffranlanzarote.com Authentic Indian cuisine at a good price.

Playa Blanca
Mid-range
The Port of Call, Faro Park, tel: 603 450 895 A wide ranging menu from British to Tex-Mex, plus daily specials. Very popular venue.
Brisa Marina, Paseo Maritimo 10, Playa Blanca, tel: 928 517206, www.restaurantebrisamarina.com Seafood restaurant; terrace overlooking the sea.
Bodegón las Tapas, Paseo Maritimo 5, Playa Blanca, tel: 928 518310. Atmospheric seafront tapas bar-restaurant.

Yaiza
Mid-range
La Era, Calle El Barranco 3, Yaiza, tel: 928 830016, www.laera.com Local food and wine in a 300-year-old farmhouse converted by Manrique, with delightful courtyards and gardens.

El Golfo
There are at least eight seafood restaurants here.

Mid-range
El Hotelito, El Golfo, tel: 928 173272, www.hotelitodelgolfo.com Tiny hotel with excellent terrace restaurant.
El Golfo, tel: 928 173147. Serves excellent paella and other fish.
Restaurante Lago Verde, Avda. El Golfo 46, tel: 928 173311. Friendly service at this seafood restaurant.

Budget
Other fish restaurants in El Golfo include **Plácido**, **Mar Azul** and **Casa Torano**.

Timanfaya National Park
Luxury
El Diablo, Islote de Hilario, Parque Nacional de Timanfaya, tel: 928 840057. Superb restaurant, designed by Manrique, in the national park. Much of the food is cooked by volcanic heat. Open for lunch only.

Femés
There are two excellent restaurants in this tiny hill village:

Mid-range
Casa Emiliano, Femés, tel: 928 830223. Good local meat dishes, including rabbit.
Balcón de Femés, tel: 928 113618. Traditional Canarian and international food. Great views from the terrace.

TOURS AND EXCURSIONS
Tours and excursions can be arranged from the resorts of Puerto del Carmen and Playa Blanca to all the main tourist attractions. The three main excursions are to the **north of the island**, including the Mirador del Río, the Jameos del Agua and the Cueva de los Verdes. A popular trip around the **south of the island** visits the Timanfaya National Park, El Golfo and La Geria. Another excursion is **In the Footsteps of César Manrique**. Some tour operators arrange day trips to the island of **Fuerteventura**, using the ferries from Playa Blanca. Local **boat trips** can be arranged from both Puerto del Carmen and Playa Blanca.

USEFUL CONTACTS
Tourist Information Offices in **Puerto del Carmen**, Avda. de las Playas, tel: 928 513351 (open Mon–Fri 10:00–14:00 and 18:00–20:00), and at **Playa Blanca**, next to the ferry terminal, tel: 928 518150 (open Mon–Fri 10:00–18:00, Sat 10:00–14:00 Oct–Jun; Mon–Fri 09:30–19:00, Sat 10:00–14:00 Jul–Sep). There is also a kiosk in the main street.

6 A Day Trip to Northern Fuerteventura

For many holiday-makers on Lanzarote, the idea of spending a day on neighbouring Fuerteventura is an attractive possibility. It provides you with the opportunity of seeing another island in the Canaries, and you can decide whether it is suitable as a future holiday destination.

Many travel companies run coach/ferry tours from Lanzarote to northern Fuerteventura, and their excellent guides present an accurate flavour of the place. It is also possible to take hired cars on the ferries to Fuerteventura and, if you have four passengers in a car, some good deals can be negotiated.

Two ferry companies operate from **Playa Blanca** in the south of Lanzarote to **Corralejo** in the north of Fuerteventura. Tickets can be purchased in the offices on the jetty at Playa Blanca. The **Fred Olsen Line** (www.fredolsen.es) ferries leave Playa Blanca daily at 07:10, 08:30, 10:00, 14:00, 16:00, 18:00 and 20:00 (Fri and Sun) returning from Corralejo at 06:30, 07:50, 09:00, 12:00, 15:00, 17:00 and 19:00 (Fri and Sun). The **Naviera Armas Line** ferries leave Playa Blanca daily at 07:00, 09:00, 11:00, 15:00, 17:00 and 19:00, returning from Corralejo at 08:00, 10:00, 14:00, 16:00, 18:00 and 20:00 (www.naviera-armas.com). For more information on ferry times, *see* page 121. Note that tickets are not interchangeable between the two lines.

FACTS ABOUT FUERTEVENTURA

Fuerteventura is the second-largest of the Canary Islands, stretching approximately 100km (62 miles) from north to

DON'T MISS

*** Corralejo Dunes Natural Park:** enjoy miles of empty beaches.
** **Betancuria:** visit the Cathedral of Santa María in the island's old capital.
* **Isla de los Lobos:** experience the peace and quiet just a boat ride from Corralejo.
* **La Oliva:** see fine 18th-century colonial houses.
* **El Cotillo and Corralejo:** try the superb seafood in these fishing settlements.

◄ *Opposite: The golden sands south of Corralejo, with Isla de los Lobos in the background.*

A DAY TRIP TO NORTHERN FUERTEVENTURA

south, with a width of 40km (25 miles) at its maximum from east to west. It is the most sparsely populated of all the Canary Islands, with just over 100,000 inhabitants, around a quarter of which live in the capital, **Puerto del Rosario**. It is also the driest of the Canary Islands, with a mere 15cm (6in) of rain falling on roughly 24 days of the year.

Fuerteventura's main products are fish, tomatoes and goat's-milk cheese. Its chief foreign earner, however, is **tourism**, with approximately 1.2 million annual visitors to the island. In the south of the island 90 per cent of the tourists are German, but the northern part of Fuerteventura is more popular with the British and Scandinavians, although many more nationalities enjoy visiting Fuerteventura.

Northern Fuerteventura

Historical Background

Fuerteventura was the second of the Canary Islands to be conquered by Europeans. The Norman **Jean de Béthencourt** and his ally **Gadifer de la Salle** landed on Fuerteventura in 1404, having previously conquered Lanzarote. They found between 6000 and 8000 Guanches, who on Fuerteventura were known as **_Majoreros_**, a word meaning 'cave-dwellers'. Spaniards later arrived in force, and the first cathedral was set up in 1426. However, the bishop resided on Gran Canaria – as did most of the landowners of the island.

For the next 300 years, Fuerteventura suffered from continuous raids by North African pirates, and it was not until the mid-19th century that it was felt safe to have the island's capital in a coastal location. The island government, **Cabildo Insular**, was set up in 1912. Then in 1927 it became part of the eastern province of the Canary Islands, along with Gran Canaria and Lanzarote.

Fuerteventura has always been politically conservative and gave considerable support to General Franco. In return, he did much to improve the infrastructure of the island. Tourism began to take off in Fuerteventura in 1966, and by the 80s and 90s tourist numbers were growing by 20 per cent a year.

▲ *Above: Fuerteventura can be seen in the distance from Playa Blanca.*

ISLAND HOPPING

The independent traveller wanting to see more than one of the islands will have little problem getting around. There are regular domestic flights linking all the islands. Contact Binter www.bintercanarios.com for details. A cheaper, but slower, way of island hopping is by **boat**, with a choice of ferries, jet foils and hydrofoils. The main companies are Trasmediterránea, Lineas Fred Olsen and Naviera Armas. Corralejo in northern Fuerteventura is connected by two ferry services to Playa Blanca in Lanzarote. Puerto del Rosario is linked by ferry to the capital, Arrecife, and to Las Palmas in Gran Canaria.

A DAY TRIP TO NORTHERN FUERTEVENTURA

▲ *Above: From a harbourside café in Corralejo, Isla de los Lobos is visible in the distance.*

A TOUR OF THE NORTH OF THE ISLAND

The following account describes a route that can be taken within a day. There is not enough time to visit all the places, so the choice depends on the visitor's interests.

Isla de los Lobos ★

As you approach Fuerteventura, the volcanic island you see on the left is **Isla de los Lobos**, an island named after the wolf seals that once lived here. Sadly, the seals are long gone, having been killed off by fishermen years ago, but the local *cabildo* has tentative plans to re-introduce them here. It is possible to take a boat from Corralejo to Isla de los Lobos, where there is a tiny fishing village called **El Puertito**, with a small restaurant and some wonderful beaches. A track can be followed all the way around the island, passing the **lighthouse** at the northern tip. It is also possible to climb up to the crater of the extinct volcano **Montaña Lobos**, standing at 127m (416ft) high – the highest point on the island.

Corralejo ★

From the ferry, **Corralejo** is seen to have a background of volcanic hills. However, unlike Lanzarote, it is over 7000 years since volcanic activity took place on Fuerteventura. Once a small fishing port, Corralejo is now a busy holiday resort, offering visitors some 15,000 beds. Although the town beach is rather small, there are miles of sand dunes to the south, where the main tourist developments are taking place. The harbour is busy, with car ferries running to Lanzarote and Las Palmas in Gran Canaria. Corralejo has a busy shopping centre, based around the main street, **Avenida Generalísimo Franco**, and the lively **Centro Atlántico**. There are good fish restaurants along the seafront and in **Plaza Felix Estavéz González**.

WHAT'S IN A NAME?

It is usually assumed that the name Fuerteventura is derived from the Spanish *el viento fuerte*, meaning strong wind. However, there might be another explanation, as Jean de Béthencourt, the Norman conqueror of the island, is said to have remarked on landing: *Que fuerte ventura*! (What a great adventure!). Certainly the original name for the island of **Herbania**, when it had luxuriant vegetation, seems hardly fitting when viewing the barren scenery of Fuerteventura today.

Parque Natural de las Dunas de Corralejo ★★★

Leave Corralejo southwards on the FV1 road to Puerto del Rosario. On the left-hand side is the **Parque Natural de las Dunas de Corralejo**, an area of sand dunes that stretches for 7km (4.5 miles) along the coast. Here, two large multi-storey hotels, **Tres Islas** and **Oliva Beach**, stand out like sore thumbs. They were built before the park was designated and no further construction allowed. The dunes are a popular haunt for naturists who are often in danger of getting sand-blasted when the winds blow strongly in summer. This is also a great spot for surfing and sailboarding, with a number of shops in Corralejo selling all the required gear.

The end of the natural park is marked, on the landward side of the road, by the hulk of the volcanic cone of **Montaña Roja**, which rises to 312m (1023ft). Sand dunes are now replaced by *malpaís*. You then reach a Dutch development, **Urbanización Parque Holandes**, which has had a chequered history. Miles from anywhere and without the benefit of a decent beach, the resort was slow to take off and the original developers went bankrupt. The continuing financial squeeze means ongoing growth is minimal.

Puerto del Rosario

The FV1 road now reaches **Puerto del Rosario**, dominated by the chimneys of the desalinization plant. The town was made the capital of Fuerteventura as recently as 1860. Before that the administrative role was taken successively by Betancuria, Antigua and La Oliva – all sited inland and much better protected from the raids of pirates. Prior to 1956 Puerto del Rosario was known as Puerto de Cabras (meaning Goat Harbour), which was hardly a suitable name for the capital of the

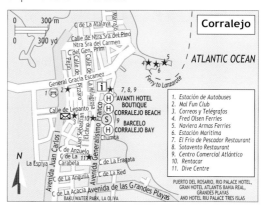

Corralejo

ATLANTIC OCEAN

1. Estación de Autobuses
2. Mal Fun Club
3. Correos y Telégrafos
4. Fred Olsen Ferries
5. Naviera Armas Ferries
6. Estación Marítima
7. El Frio de Pescador Restaurant
8. Sotavento Restaurant
9. Centro Comercial Atlántico
10. Rentacar
11. Dive Centre

AVANTI HOTEL BOUTIQUE
CORRALEJO BEACH
BARCELO
CORRALEJO BAY

PUERTO DEL ROSARIO, RIO PALACE HOTEL, GRAN HOTEL ATLANTIS BAHIA REAL, GRANDES PLAYAS AND HOTEL RIU PALACE TRES ISLAS

BAKU WATER PARK, LA OLIVA

A DAY TRIP TO NORTHERN FUERTEVENTURA

Fuerteventura's hard-pressed farmers have recently found that the island's climate is ideal for the production of the spiky, cactus-like plant known as **aloe vera** (*Aloe barbadensis miller*). Its healing properties were well known to the ancient Egyptians, who called it the plant of immortality, but it wasn't until the 1970s that it became popular in the health industry. The yellow juice in the plant is packed with antioxidant vitamins. It can be drunk like a fruit juice to relieve digestion problems, and applied to the skin as treatment for eczema and rheumatism. The more research that is carried out on aloe vera, the more benefits there seem to be and there are few, if any, side effects. Fuerteventura's farmers are, not surprisingly, increasing their production.

island. It began to develop as a port in the 19th century and continues to be the main commercial centre of Fuerteventura today, with a number of industrial estates in the suburbs. It was also the home, for many years, of the **Spanish Foreign Legion**, who came here when Spanish Sahara gained its independence. The presence of so many soldiers fuelled the development of the red-light district of Barrio Chino, which is now being cleaned up.

Today, Puerto del Rosario has a population of 28,350 people, many of whom are immigrants from Andalucía and Galicia who work in the tourist and construction industries. Although it is the dominant settlement on the island, it makes few concessions to tourists. The small number of hotels in the town cater mainly to business people and the town beach, **Playa Blanca**, is used largely by locals.

Vistors on a one-day trip to Fuerteventura might wish to give Puerto del Rosario a miss, but it is a good shopping centre. The main shopping area runs from the **Plaza de España** on the promenade along **Avenida León y Castillo**. The only other item of interest in Puerto del Rosario is the Casa Museo Unamuno, based on the work of the Spanish poet and academic Miguel de Unamuno (1864–1936), who was exiled to Fuerteventura in the 1920s. Open Mon–Fri 09:00–14:00. Free entry.

▶▶ *Opposite: A restored windmill reminds visitors to the area that this was once a fertile valley.*
▶ *Right: The river valley that runs through the centre of Betancuria is dry for much of the year.*

HEADING INLAND

Take the FV20 road inland, and head towards Antigua. This route passes through the **Valley of the Windmills**. Up until the early 19th century this valley was fertile, and large amounts of wheat and maize were grown here – hence the windmills, which were used to grind the corn to make *gofio*. However, during the 1800s there was a prolonged period of drought, which caused the ground water to sink and become very salty. Many farmers emigrated to Latin America, and today the only agriculture in the valley is the production of aloe vera. Just outside **Antigua** a large restored windmill dominates the skyline. This marks a sort of museum village known as the **Museo del Queso Majorero** (Majorero Cheese Museum). As well as the windmill, which still produces *gofio*, there are displays about the said cheese, studios where craftsmen demonstrate their work, and a gift shop.

Antigua *

As its name suggests, Antigua is an ancient settlement. It was founded in 1485 and was briefly the capital of the island in the early 19th century, before handing over the role to La Oliva. Head for the main square and the parish church, the **Iglesia de Nuestra Señora de Antigua**. It dates from 1785 and has a fine *Mudéjar* ceiling. Antigua today is a rather sleepy town, well known as the craft centre of the island. There is an annual *feria* that concentrates on arts and crafts, and a regular craft market. The local cultural centre trains young people in the traditional music and dance of the island.

From Antigua, head westwards on the FV30 towards Betancuria. The road goes over a pass, from where there are fine views at the **Mirador de Morro Velosa** looking over the whole of the north of the island. Here there are two fine statues of Guanche chiefs. From here the road drops down into the village of Betancuria.

LIFE IN THE DESERT

It might be thought that a barren place such as Fuerteventura should be largely devoid of wildlife, but this is not the case. The island's shoreline, particularly at migration time, can be rich in gulls and wading birds. The dunes and barren gravel plains are home to a variety of desert birds, more typical of North Africa. These include the houbara bustard, the black-bellied sand grouse, the cream-coloured courser and the trumpeter bullfinch. Mammals are almost non-existent, with the notable exception of the introduced ground squirrel, which is thriving on the island.

A DAY TRIP TO NORTHERN FUERTEVENTURA

▲ *Above: Betancuria's charming church was consecrated as a cathedral in 1426.*

Betancuria ★★

This idyllic village takes its name from the Norman conqueror **Jean de Béthencourt**. He landed on the west coast of the island, but became frustrated by the frequent raids of pirates. In 1405 he decided to push inland and set up his capital at Betancuria, where there was a permanently flowing stream, lush vegetation and a greater degree of security. It was to remain the administrative centre of the island for over 400 years. The village church, the **Iglesia de Santa María**, was consecrated as a cathedral in 1426, although no bishop has ever resided there. Betancuria's remote location proved no hindrance to pirates, however, and in 1593 a band of men led by the North African Jaban, attacked and set fire to the town, destroying the cathedral. It was not rebuilt for a hundred years. The cathedral has a beautiful wooden *Mudéjar* ceiling, made of wood from Tenerife and supported by delicate round stone arches. The *reredos* behind the altar is dripping with gold leaf and includes the Virgen del la Peña, the patron saint of both the town and the island. Look, too, for the bishop's head carved in wood and the *Last Judgement* painting by the baptistry in the southwest corner. The sacristy, to the left of the altar, contains some church silver and vestments. There is no organ in the church – nowadays it is more of a museum than a place of worship. Don't worry if you cannot gain immediate entry to the church – the lady curator who has the key commutes between the church and the nearby museum. On the far side of the small church square is the **Casa Santa María**, a restored town house that is now an excellent restaurant. There is a shop in the basement selling local ceramics and craft items.

Close by is a small museum, the **Museo de Artesania**, which has an excellent multi-vision show on the island of Fuerteventura. Among the displays are traditional agricultural implements, including ploughs, camel seats and harnessing, as well as a collection of local herbs and spices. Open Tuesday—Saturday 10:00—18:00.

In the main street, on the far side of the normally dry river valley, is the town's **Museo Arqueológico**, which contains a number of archaeological finds from Guanche times. It is open from Tuesday to Saturday 10:00—18:00. On the northern edge of the town is the ruined **Convento de San Buenaventura**, a Franciscan monastery dating back to the early days of the Conquest. It closed down in the 19th century and much of its stonework was stolen for building material. There has been some restoration of the monastery's church, but it is usually locked up.

A few kilometres south of Betancuria is the Valley of Palms leading to the attractive village of **Pájara**, with a pretty tree-lined main street. Said to be the most affluent village on the island, Pájara boasts a superb church, **Nuestra Señora de la Regla**. Admire the red sandstone doorway decorated with Aztec-style symbols. The interior has two naves, each with its high altar, but unfortunately you are unlikely to see them as the church is invariably firmly locked — the result of a theft of religious valuables. It is said that even the priest is not allowed to have the key! Opposite the church is a complex water-pumping arrangement involving a wheel that was once operated by a camel. It is worth wandering through the shady park at the side of the church where a bridge crosses a dry river bed festooned with bougainvillea and other flowering shrubs.

With more goats than people living on Fuerteventura it would be a pity not to visit a **goat farm**. There is a convenient one on the road a few kilometres south of Betancuria, which is very child-friendly. Here you can see goats in their indoor pens and watch them being milked, while ducks and chickens wander around the place. There is a small restaurant and shop, where the locally made goat's-milk cheese and honey can be sampled.

GOATS GALORE

Foreign drivers in Fuerteventura are often surprised to see road signs warning them of the likelihood of cows or deer straying across the road. Surely a mistake? Yes. What the motorist should be looking out for are **goats**. However, there is no international road sign for a goat, so a cow or a deer motif has to suffice. There are reputed to be some 68,000 goats on the island of Fuerteventura and they are raised for the production of goat's milk, which is then made into cheese. Unfortunately, goats eat any vegetation and this defoliation of the island has contributed to the low rainfall resulting in increased aridity — a climatic vicious circle.

▼ Below: The entrance to one of the many goat farms on the island of Fuerteventura.

A DAY TRIP TO NORTHERN FUERTEVENTURA

EMBROIDERY STYLES

There are numerous craft industries to be found in the Canary
Islands and one of the most
widespread is **embroidery** and
lace-making. The centre of this
craft on Fuerteventura is the
northern village of **Lajares**. Here,
there is an embroidery school
where you can watch women
learning the skill, and buy some
of their products. It is possible to tell which island an item
comes from by the pattern and
design shown. If it comes from
Lanzarote, for example, it will
always show a volcanic crater.
Fuerteventura always features a
windmill, and the designs from La
Palma show the poinsettia flower.

Leave Betancuria northwards on the FV30, passing the
Mirador de Morro Velosa and then turning along the **Valle de
Santa Inés**. The valley, the village and its church were named
after one Inés Peraza, who provided money for the church to
be dedicated to the saint of her own name in the 16th century.

Head now along the FV207 towards the village of **Tefía**
where you will find **Ecomuseo de la Alcogida**, an **open-
air museum**. Old farm buildings and houses have been
reconstructed and reassembled here, along with restored
windmills, straw 'ice houses' and assorted ovens. Open
Tue–Sat 10:00–18:00; entry fee.

Continuing north, now on the FV10, the road swings
between two mountains. On the right is **Montaña La Muda**,
which at 689m (2260ft) is the highest mountain in northern
Fuerteventura. On the left we see **Montaña Quemada**, which
rises to 294m (964ft). This is the site of the **Monumento
a Don Miguel de Unamuno**, the poet and academic who
was exiled to Fuerteventura for many years in the early
20th century.

La Oliva ★

The tour now approaches the town of **La Oliva**, yet another
of the inland settlements that has served as capital of
Fuerteventura. It dates from the early 17th century when
it was a residence for the island's governors. Sadly, many
of the town houses from
those times seem in need
of renovation. Dominating
the town is the parish
church of **Nuestra Señora
de Candelaria**. Its square
tower of dark volcanic rock
contrasts strongly with the
whitewashed walls. Inside
there is a *Mudéjar* ceiling
and some trompe l'oeil
decoration. Of the numer-
ous town houses, the most

▼ *Below: A bread oven
alongside one of the farm
buildings at the open-air
eco-museum at Tefía.*

impressive is the **Casa de los Coroneles**, which was the home of the island's military governors and dates from 1708. Look over the main door at the coat of arms, which belonged to the Cabrera-Béthencourt family, descendents of the original Norman conqueror of the island. Opposite the Casa de los Coroneles is the **Centro de Arte Canario**, tel: 928 568233, based in another town house, the Casa Mané. The paintings here are modern, as are the sculptures, which are displayed in a courtyard.

▲ *Above: A needlewoman at work in the embroidery school at Lajares.*

Continue northwards to the village of **Lajares**. As the village is approached, the attention is drawn to two well-preserved windmills dating back to the 19th century. On the right is a more substantial 'male' *molino* (mill), while on the left is the more flimsy timber structured 'female' *molina* – making an interesting comparison. Lajares is also famous for its embroidery. Next to the windmills is the **Artesania Lajares**, where it is possible to watch women at work embroidering and lace-making. You can buy their products at the shop.

If you have enough time, a diversion can be made from Lajares to the west-coast fishing village of **El Cotillo**. Once noted for its smuggling activities, El Cotillo has recently been discovered by tourists. There are some good sea-food restaurants around the old harbour, which is the most picturesque part of the village. The only monument of interest is the **Castillo del Tostón**, just to the south of the port. It was built in 1743 to help repel the medley of pirates who plagued the coast. The fort is round and tapers skywards. Originally, troops lived on the ground floor, while the upper level was used for water storage. There has been some renovation, and the castle is open to the public. From El Cotillo, return to Lajares and head back to the ferry at Corralejo on the FV101.

CHIPMUNKS

Some years ago the ground squirrel or Moroccan chipmunk was introduced to Fuerteventura. Here they have thrived to such an extent that many now consider them to be pests. These enduring little mammals do not live in trees but prefer homes in holes in the ground or under rocks. The best places to see the chipmunks are at the miradors in central Fuerteventura, where the arrival of a few tourists will bring scores of them out of their holes. Produce a few sunflower seeds and they will eat out of your hand. One curious result of the introduction of chipmunks has been the drastic reduction in rabbit numbers, possibly because the chipmunks graze on the rabbits' food.

NORTHERN FUERTEVENTURA AT A GLANCE

BEST TIME TO VISIT
Fuerteventura is an all-year-round destination, with not a great deal of climatic variety. If any rain falls it will be in the winter months, when the evenings can be cool. Summers are hotter, drier and windier.

GETTING THERE
It is possible to fly from Arrecife to Puerto del Rosario, but the short distance and the high cost involved do not make this a very sensible option. Most visitors from Lanzarote take a ferry, either from Playa Blanca to Corralejo or from Arrecife to Puerto del Rosario.

GETTING AROUND
Many visitors explore northern Fuerteventura on a coach excursion. Others prefer to bring their own hired car over from Lanzarote. Another possibility is to come over on the ferry as a foot passenger and hire a car in Corralejo. Either way, visitors find driving conditions convenient and similar to those in Lanzarote, with clear signposting and good road surfaces. Scooters and motorcycles can also be hired in Corralejo, as can mountain bikes for those visitors who have a limited budget or more adventurous inclinations.

WHERE TO STAY
Most visitors from Lanzarote are on a day trip, so accommo-dation is seldom considered. It is possible, however, to come to the island for a few days, but book accommodation well beforehand, particularly at more popular times of year.

Luxury
Gran Hotel Atlantis Bahia Real, Avda. Grandes Playas, Correlejo, tel: 928 536444, fax: 928 537575, www.atlantis bahiareal.com Large luxury hotel complex on the beach.
Hotel Rui Palace Tres Islas, Avda. Grandes Playas 35660, Corralejo, tel: 928 535700, fax: 928 535858, www.riu.com Probably the best hotel on the island, run by the Riu group, on the beachfront in the beautiful natural park.

Mid-range
Club Hotel Rui Oliva Beach Resort, Avda. Grandes Playas 35660, Corralejo, tel: 928 535334, fax: 928 866154, www.riu.com Family-friendly hotel with an Olympic-sized pool, situated on the beach.
Avanti Hotel Boutique, Avda. Maritima, Corralejo, tel/fax: 928 867523, www.avantihotel boutique.com Adult only hotel in the heart of the town.

Budget
Hotel Rural Mahoh, Sitio de Juan Bello, Villaverde, La Oliva tel: 928 868050, fax: 928 868612, www.mahoh.com Small rustic hotel with on-site restaurant.
Playa Park Club, Calle Lanzarote 4, Correlejo, tel: 928 867090, www.playa parkcorralejo.com Mid-sized family-friendly hotel, good range of facilities.

WHERE TO EAT
Luxury
El Andaluz, Calle Ballena, Corralejo, tel: 676 705878. Long-standing up-market favourite. European cuisine.
Casa Santa María, Plaza de la Iglesia, Betancuria, tel: 928 878282, www.casa santamaria.net One of the best on the island, but quite expensive.

Mid-range
For good seafood in Corralejo, try the following restaurants along the waterfront: **Marquesina I** and **II, El Frio de Pescador** and **Sotavento**. **La Mamma**, Anzuelo 5, Corralejo, tel: 928 537573, www.pizzerialamamma.net is the best place in town for steak lovers.
Casa Marcos, Carretera General, Villaverde, tel: 928 868285. Excellent local ingre-dients for tapas and traditional Canarian dishes.
Restaurant Mahoh Sitio de Juan Bello, Villaverde, La Oliva tel: 928 868050, www.mahoh. com Excellent restaurant serv-ing seasonal Canarian dishes.

Budget
Baobab Juice Bar Casa Vegetariana, Calle Jose Segura Torres 14, Corralejo, tel: 602 624532. Excellent meat free options and refreshing snacks.

Tours and Excursions

Most travel agents in Lanzarote arrange coach excursions in northern Fuerteventura, visiting **Corralejo**, **Antigua**, **Betancuria** and **Lajares**, as well as a goat farm. Tours can be arranged from Corralejo around the north of the island and also out to **Isla de los Lobos**. Contact Ultramar Express, Calle El Arado 17, El Matorral, Puerto del Rosario, tel: 928 543461, www.ultra maexpresstransport.com For personal **taxi tours** of the north of the island, contact Radio Taxis Puerto del Rosario, tel: 928 850216, www.taxisfuerte ventura.es Other activities include dune walks, boat trips and deap-sea angling. For safaris on **quads** and **dune buggies** contact X-Quad Fuerteventura, Calle La Acacia 2, Correlejo, tel: 928 535076.

Further South: Fuerteventura is only 100km (62 miles) in length, so it is possible for day-trippers from Lanzarote to see something of the south of the island, easily done with a hired car. South of Puerto del Rosario is the resort of **El Castillo**, which boasts an old fort, a yachting harbour and an attractive sandy bay. Don't miss the fishing village of **Tarajalejo**, with good seafood restaurants and an art gallery. The major resort in the south is **Jandía Playa**, with impressive white sand beaches. Inland, the main settlement is **Tuineje**, an agricultural village with a Moorish feel.

Useful Contacts

Tourist Information Offices:
Puerto del Rosario, Avda. Reyes de España, tel: 928 850110, www.turismo-puerto delrosario.org Open Mon–Fri 08:00–14:00. A kiosk at the airport is open daily (09:00–20:00).
Corralejo, Avda. Maritima 2, tel: 928 866235. Open Mon–Fri 09:00–14:00, 16:30–19:30. Also tourist information available at the ferry port.

Ferry services:
Naviera Armas, tel: 928 867080 in Corralejo, tel: 928 851542 in Puerto del Rosario or call centre tel: 902 456500, www.navieraarmas.com Naviera runs ferries between the two ports seven times daily, the voyage taking around 35 mins.
Fred Olsen Shipping Line, tel: 902 100107 or 928 495040, or for general information tel: 902 100107, www.fredolsen.es Operates a fast catamaran six times a day, the journey taking around 20 mins. Tickets are not interchangeable between the two companies. Both ships take vehicles. Fred Olsen operates a free connecting bus service from the main resorts to Playa Blanca.
Trasmediterránea runs a ferry service between Arrecife and Puetro del Rosario. Three services a week and the journey takes around three hours. For details tel: 928 824930 (Arrecife) and tel: 902 850877 (Puerto del Rosario), www.trasmediterranea.es

There is plenty of opportunity for **water sports** at Corralejo: for **diving**, contact Dive Centre Corralejo, tel: 928 535906, www.divecentrecorralejo.com for **windsurfing**, contact Flag Beach Windsurf Centre and for **deep-sea fishing**, contact Pez Velero, tel: 928 866389, www.flagbeach.com
Children will appreciate the **Acua Fun Park** in Corralejo, open daily from mid-June to mid-Sep 10:00–18:00, reduced hours for the rest of the year, www.acuafunpark.com
For **car hire** services, contact **Cicar**, Centro Comercial Atlántico, Avenida Generalísimo Franco, tel: 928 822900, www.cicar.com and **Hertz**, Hotel Correlejo Beach, Avenida Nuestra Senora del Carmen, tel: 928 535842, www.hertz.com
For hiring and/or touring on **mountain bikes** contact Easy Riders Atlantis Fuerteventura Resort, Corralejo, tel: 928 867005, www.easyriders-bikecenter.com
Some informative **websites:** www.fuerteventura.com and www.sunnyfuerteventura.com

Shopping

Craftwork typical of Fuerteventura can be found in a number of places in the northern part of the island. Artisans can be seen at work, for example, at the **embroidery** school in Lajares. Also highly recommended is Casa Santa María in Betancuria.

Travel Tips

TOURIST INFORMATION

The **Spanish Tourist Board** has offices in the USA, Canada and a host of non-English-speaking countries. In the UK, the address is: Spanish National Tourist Office, 6th Floor, 64 North Row, London, W1K 7DE, tel: 020 317 2040, www.tourspain.co.uk Other websites providing additional information: www.icanarias.com www.lanzarote.com www.discoverlanzarote.com www.spain.info On Lanzarote itself, the tourist authority is based at the government offices, Cabilda Insular, Blas Cabrera Felipe, 35500, Arrecife, tel: 928 811762, fax: 928 800080, www.turismolanzarote.com The main tourist information office in **Arrecife** is on the waterfront at Parque José Ramírez Cerdá, tel: 928 813174. Open Mon–Fri 09:30–17:00, Sat 10:00–13:00.
Arrecife Airport (Terminal One) has a tourist office that is open during the busier times; tel: 928 820704.
At **Puerto del Carmen** the tourist office occupies a distinctive octagonal wooden building on the seafront in Avenida de las Playas, tel: 928 513351.
Open Mon–Fri (10:00–14:00 and 18:00–20:00). There is

also a small tourist office at **Playa Blanca**, situated near the ferry terminal, tel: 928 518150. Open Mon–Fri 10:00–18:00, Sat 10:00–14:00 Oct–June; Mon–Fri 09:30–19:00, Sat 10:00–14:00 Jul–Sep.
Costa Teguise office is at Avenida Islas Canarias, tel: 928 592542. Open Mon–Fri 09:30–17:00, Sat–Sun 10:00–15:30.

ENTRY REQUIREMENTS

Visitors from Britain, USA, Canada, New Zealand and Australia must have a valid **passport**. If staying for longer than three months a **visa** is required from the Spanish Embassy in their native country. Anyone losing their passport should contact their consulate. Most of these are in Las Palmas, but the British Consulate has a representative available on the island. Contact them through the Las Palmas office.

CUSTOMS

The Canary Islands, despite being part of Spain, are not considered a member of the EU. The EU abolished the duty-free allowances in 1999, but at the time of writing certain limits remain on goods taken in and out of Lanzarote. There are advantages and disadvantages. For example, there are still bargains to be

had at the airport's duty-free shop. Restrictions on the **duty-free allowance** are one litre of spirits; two litres of fortified wine and two litres of table wine; 200 cigarettes or 50 cigars; and gifts up to the value of £390 sterling.

HEALTH REQUIREMENTS

No vaccinations are necessary unless coming from a country with smallpox, typhoid or yellow fever. There is no malaria in the Canary Islands and mosquitoes are usually rare. Visitors from EU countries should take the European Health Insurance Card (EHIC), as it affords a degree of free medical treatment, although it is no substitute for a good medical insurance.

GETTING THERE

By air: The only **airport** serving Lanzarote is located south of **Arrecife** (Airport code ACE). It has two terminals: T2 is mostly used for inter-island flights, so most international tourists will arrive at T1. Buses and taxis connect the airport with Arrecife to the north and with the resorts to the south. There are international flights every day of the week. Scheduled flights arrive from the UK (mainly the 'no frills' airlines), Spain and Germany, but there is a strong dependence on charter flights controlled by tour operators. UK charter flights run from no fewer than 17 regional airports, while there are also routes from 10 other European countries, indicating the popularity of Lanzarote as a tourist destination.

By sea: The only ferry (for both car and foot passengers) from Europe to Lanzarote is operated by Trasmediterránea (tel: 928 824930). It sails from Cádiz on the Spanish mainland and runs twice a week calling in at Santa Cruz and Las Palmas before proceeding to Arrecife on the return journey. Book well in advance for summer sailings.

WHAT TO PACK

With such a mild climate throughout the year, there is no need to pack heavy clothing. A light jumper and windproof jacket are useful during the evenings or if trips to the breezier northern part of the island are planned in the winter months. For beach holidays, some light sandals are recommended as the volcanic sand can become very hot underfoot. Stronger footwear is needed for hiking over the volcanoes and badlands. The sun can be strong throughout the year, so sunglasses and a hat are advisable. Don't forget sun protection cream, and remember that light cotton clothes are most comfortable. Shorts and swimming costumes are essential. Smarter casual wear is needed for the evenings, particularly in the

hotels and more expensive restaurants. Beachwear is unacceptable when visiting churches. *Lanzaroteños* themselves generally dress casually, except on more formal occasions. Lanzarote, with its clear light and stunning scenery, is a highly photogenic island and most visitors will want to bring a camera or camcorder.

MONEY MATTERS

Currency: The Euro was introduced in January 2002. It is split into 100 cents. Coins come in denominations of one, two, five, 10, 20, and 50 cents, and 1 and 2 Euro coins. Notes are issued in five, 10, 50, 100, 200 and 500 Euros.

Currency Exchange: Travellers' cheques and foreign currency can be cashed at banks, exchange outlets and hotels. Remember to have your passport available. There are automatic cash dispensers (ATMs) in all the main resorts, using a variety of languages.

Banks: Finding a bank is not a problem, although service may be slow. They are open on weekdays from 09:00 to 14:00 and on Saturdays from 09:00 to 13:00.

Credit Cards: The major credit cards are accepted throughout Lanzarote in most shops, hotels and exchange offices (but not at all restaurants).

Tipping: A service charge is added to hotel and restaurant bills, so tipping is a matter of personal choice.

ROAD SIGNS

Traffic symbols in Lanzarote are those used throughout the EU and they are internationally recognized. The road signs include:

Alto • Stop
Camino Cerrado • Road Closed
Ceda el paso • Give way
Circunvalación • Bypass
Curva Peligrosa • Dangerous Bend
Derecha • Right
Derecho • Straight On
Despacio • Slow
Derrumbes en la Vía • Rockfalls on the road
Dirección Unica • One way
Izquierdo • Left
No Adelantar • No Overtaking
No Estacionar/Parquero • No Parking
No Hay Paso • No Entrance
Peligro • Danger
Reduzca Velocidad • Reduce Speed
Salida • Exit
Semáforo • Traffic Lights
Trabajos en la Vía • Roadworks

ACCOMMODATION

Most of the accommodation on Lanzarote is geared to package tours, which means that the individual traveller who just turns up might find hotels and apartment blocks fully booked. It is best to arrange accommodation before arriving on the island. There is a vast range of **hotels** from luxury establishments to modest *pensiónes*. **Aparthotels** have similar facilities, but have some

self-catering rooms.
Apartments far outnumber hotels and are cheaper, but beware that prices may be per room, even if not fully occupied. *Pensiónes* are in short supply, apart from a handful in Arrecife, and the island is not really a good location for the independent budget traveller. *Casas rurales* are converted farmhouses or village properties that make an attractive option for those who wish to get away from the bustle of the large resorts. They mainly offer bed and breakfast.

EATING OUT

A wide range of **restaurants**, especially in the main resorts, provide for every need and palate. The resort restaurants cater mainly for tourists and so provide international food. There are usually printed menus posted outside the premises, often with a national flag representing each language, and in some cases photos of the various dishes. Fast-food restaurants abound, such as KFC, McDonalds and numerous pizza outlets. Restaurants specializing in food from Italy, Thailand, India, France, Mexico and many other countries ensure that the visitor has a wide choice. To experience genuine Canarian food head inland, away from the large resorts, or to the capital Arrecife. One of the joys of eating out in the Canary Islands is to sample food in the many **seafood restaurants**, which provide a variety of fresh shellfish and fish, usually at reasonable prices. **Cafés and bars** are found everywhere and many provide *tapas* with drinks. A cheap way of eating is to order the meal of the day (*menu del día*), which usually consists of a starter, main course, dessert and a drink.

TRANSPORT

Air: There are inter-island flights from Lanzarote to all the other Canary Islands. Binter is the regional carrier (www.bintercanarias.com).
Ferries: All the islands in the group are served by regular ferry services, run by Compania Trasmediterránea, Lineas Fred Olsen and Naviera Armas.

Buses: Known by the South American name *guaguas* (pronounced *wahwahs*), the buses provide a patchy service around the island.
Car Hire: Car-hire rates on Lanzarote are just about the cheapest in Europe and with a good, well-signposted road system the rental of a car can add much to the enjoyment of a holiday. Most of the international rental firms have an office at the airport and also deliver vehicles to hotels. Local car-hire firms will be cheaper, and the following are efficient and have good back-up in case of emergency: **Autos A Cabrera** (www.autosacabrera.com), **Plus Car** (www.autospluscar.com) and **Autos Feber** (www.autosfeber.es); all three have offices in the main resorts. Drivers should be careful, as there are a large number of hire cars on the roads of Lanzarote and a dawdling convoy of such cars can drive local drivers to distraction when they are trying to get to work. Although there are many (often complex) roundabouts on the island, it is a curious fact that there are no traffic lights whatsoever!
Driving hints: In Lanzarote you drive on the right, overtake left and give way on roundabouts to traffic coming from the left. Carry your driving licence and passport (or a photocopy) when driving, as the police can demand to see them. Seat belts should be worn at all times, including those in the rear seats. It is prohibited to use a cell phone when driving

From	To	Multiply By
Millimetres	Inches	0.0394
Metres	Yards	1.0936
Metres	Feet	3.281
Kilometres	Miles	0.6214
Square kilometres	Square miles	0.386
Hectares	Acres	2.471
Litres	Pints	1.760
Kilograms	Pounds	2.205
Tonnes	Tons	0.984

CONVERSION CHART

To convert Celsius to Fahrenheit: x 9 ÷ 5 + 32

and to throw objects out of windows. Police can impose on-the-spot fines to non-resident drivers, but there is a 20 per cent discount if the fine is paid immediately. Speed limits are 120kph (75mph) on motorways, 100kph (62mph) on dual carriageways, and 90kph (55mph) on other roads. There is a speed limit of 60kph (35mph) in built-up areas. **Parking** can be difficult in Arrecife and the larger resorts, where parking meters and pay-and-display areas are marked by blue lines. **Petrol stations** are widespread along the main roads and the majority accept credit cards. Fuel is cheaper than in the mainland and the rest of Europe. It is advisable to have a good map of Lanzarote if driving around the island. The *Globetrotter Travel Map* that accompanies this guide is recommended.
Taxis: Lanzarote's taxis are good value by European standards. They are generally modern Mercedes and show a plate with the letters SP (*servicio publico* – public service). They are metered for short journeys; for longer trips you should negotiate the fare with the driver. A green light means the taxi is free for hire.

Business Hours
Offices, post offices and most shops are open between 09:00 and 13:00, and, after the siesta period, between 16:00 and 19:00. On Saturdays opening hours are from 09:00 to 13:00. Food stores and supermarkets (*super-mercados*) may open for longer periods, while some shops in the tourist resorts may open on Sundays.

Time Difference
Lanzarote, along with the rest of the Canary Islands, maintains Greenwich Mean Time in the winter months, so there is a one-hour time difference with the continent. Clocks are one hour ahead in summer.

Communications
Telephones: If making an international call from Lanzarote, dial 00 first, then the country code, followed by the area code (omitting the first 0) and then the number. If dialling Lanzarote from abroad, the country code is 34 – the same as the rest of Spain. There many distinctive blue telephone booths, which take both phone cards and cash. These cards (*tarjetas telefónicas*) can be bought at post offices, tobacconists, shops and hotels. If making long-distance calls, it is best to use the large cabins or *locutorios*. You pay on leaving and credit cards are accepted.
Mobile phones generally work well in Lanzarote.
Post: Post boxes (*buzons*) are yellow. Stamps (*sellos*) are sold at post offices (*oficinas de correos*), tobacconists (*estancos*) and shops that sell postcards. Post offices open during normal office hours. Allow a week for a card to reach Europe, 10 days to North America and two weeks for Australia, New Zealand and South Africa.
Fax: Most hotels provide a free fax service, but expect to pay a fee for the service in a post office or tourist information centre

Electricity
The electric current is 220 volts for shaving sockets. Plugs have two round pins in line with most of Europe. Bring adapters for appliances and buy them before leaving home, as it is unlikely you'll find them here.

Weights and Measures
The metric system is used in both Lanzarote and the rest of the Canary Islands.

Useful Phrases

Yes, No • *Si, No*
Please • *Por favor*
Thank you • *Gracias*
Hello • *Hola*
Goodbye • *Adiós*
See you later • *Hasta Luego*
My name is... • *Me Llamo...*
Do you speak English? • *¿Habla (usted) Inglés?*
You're welcome • *De nada*
I don't speak Spanish • *No hablo Español*
How much is...? • *¿Cuánto cuesta...?*
Do you have...? • *¿Tiene...?*
Please speak more slowly • *Hablé más despacio, por favor*
Where is? • *¿Dónde está?*
What time does it arrive/ leave? • *¿A qué hora llega/sale?*
Do you have anything cheaper? • *¿No tiene algo más barato?*
Is there...? • *¿Hay...?*
Please fill the tank • *Llénelo del todo, por favor*
Is there a hotel near here? • *¿Hay un hotel por aqui?*

TRAVEL TIPS

HEALTH SERVICES
Visitors from EU countries should bring their European Health Insurance Card (EHIC) with them; this should be obtained before travelling. This card does not cover medical prescriptions or dental treatment. Lanzarote has some good hospitals and private clinics with English-speaking staff. Hotels usually provide the name of an English-speaking doctor (*medico*). Freephone doctor, tel: 900 707 777.

Minor medical problems can usually be solved by visiting a pharmacy (*farmacia*). *Farmacias* are open during normal business hours and distinguished by a green cross. In larger towns, at least one pharmacy will be open after hours and a duty rota is displayed in the window.

HEALTH PRECAUTIONS
Most visitors to Lanzarote experience few health problems. The biggest danger is over-exposure to the sun, resulting in **sunburn** and **dehydration**. Sunbathing should be taken steadily and sunblocks should be applied generously. Wear a sun hat and good sunglasses – avoid exposure during the hottest parts of the day. Note that sunburn is possible even if there is a layer of cloud.

PERSONAL SAFETY
Crime is relatively low in Lanzarote, even in Arrecife. Local authorities realize that adverse crime figures can affect tourism, which means that the police keep a high profile in order to keep the island safe. Most visitors will not feel threatened, but nevertheless petty crime does exist.

EMERGENCIES
Dial the **pan-European** emergency number **112** for all problems. A multi-language staff will then send the appropriate help.

ETIQUETTE
Topless sunbathing is common at beaches and around pools, but full nudity is frowned upon and is only tolerated in certain remote locations, such as the Papagayo beaches. Beachwear is not acceptable when visiting churches.

GOOD READING

Concepción, José Luis (1984) *The Guanches – survivors and their descendents*. A sympathetic account of the early inhabitants of the Canary Islands. Ediciones Graficolor, La Laguna, Tenerife.
Fernández-Armesto, Felipe (1982) *The Canary Islands After the Conquest*. A specialized history of the islands in the 16th century. Clarendon, Oxford.
Sánchez-Pinto, Lázaro and de Saá, Lucas (1993) *Flora of the Canary Islands*. A handbook and map in folder form. Ediciones Turquesa, Santa Cruz, Tenerife.
Walker, Ann and Larry *Pleasures of the Canary Islands: Wine, Food, Beauty, Mystery*. Particularly good on cooking. Hardback.
Clarke, Tony and Collins, David (1996) *A Birdwatcher's Guide to the Canary Islands*. Prion, UK.

INDEX